HARBRACE COLLEGE WORKBOOK

FORM 7B

HARBRACE COLLEGE WORKBOOK

FORM **7** B

Sheila Y. Graham

Galveston College

**in consultation with
Mrs. John C. Hodges**

Harcourt Brace Jovanovich, Inc.

New York / Chicago / San Francisco / Atlanta

Contents

PUNCTUATION

EFFECTIVE SENTENCES

EFFECTIVE COMPOSITIONS

Preface

To the Instructor

This book is frankly utilitarian. It begins with sentence analysis and stresses the basic principles of the clear English sentence. It keeps grammatical terms to a minimum, introducing only those principles most useful in writing.

Arrangement   The materials are arranged under numbers **1** to **31**—omitting **8**, which is covered in the preface to the student—to parallel the first thirty-one sections of the *Harbrace College Handbook,* Seventh Edition. But these materials may be used to supplement any handbook, or they may be used independently. The explanatory pages preceding each section enable the book to stand on its own. The order in which the materials should be studied, as well as the speed with which they should be covered, will naturally be determined by the instructor in the light of the first written work or of diagnostic tests. The needs of the class will determine whether an assignment will consist of the normal single exercise, of only a part of one, or—at the other extreme—of several exercises. Some of the exercises can be done orally in class.

Exercises   The subject matter of the exercises concerns male-female relationships, one of today's most frequently discussed topics. Thus the exercises give the student a perspective on a current subject while he is working to improve his composition.

The Dictionary   One reason for varying the order of the exercises may be the need at the opening of the course for a review of the uses of the dictionary. Unless each member of the class owns a good dictionary and knows how to use it effectively for spelling, pronunciation, meanings of words, and other information, the first assignment may very well be Exercise 19-1, Using the Dictionary.

Spelling   Ignorance of the correct spelling of ordinary words is now, and will probably continue to be, the one universally accepted sign of the uneducated man. After the student has reached senior high school or college, he cannot count on much class time being devoted to spelling. Correct spelling is then his own responsibility. He can make steady improvement in his spelling by listing and mastering every word he has misspelled. The list should be carefully kept in the blanks at the end of this book. If the list grows to considerable length before the class comes to Section **18**, the student can further improve his spelling by analyzing his own misspellings in connection with Exercises 18-1 through 18-5. Any poor speller who carefully follows the spelling program provided in this book will be pleased with the marked improvement in his spelling.

Writing The written work of the course will enable the student to carry over into the sentences of paragraphs and longer papers the principles of good writing mastered through the sentences of the workbook. To correct his written work the student may be referred to the explanatory sections, each of which has a number and a symbol derived from the *Harbrace College Handbook,* Seventh Edition.

To the Student

Preparation of Your Manuscript

Materials Unless you are given other instructions, use standard theme paper, 8½ by 11 inches, with lines about half an inch apart. Use black or blue-black ink. For typewritten themes use regular typewriter paper, 8½ by 11 inches. Submit typewritten themes only if you do your own typing.

Arrangement on the Page Leave sufficient margins—about an inch and a half at left and top, an inch at right and bottom—to prevent a crowded appearance. The ruled lines on theme paper indicate the proper margins at left and top. In typewritten themes use double spacing. Indent the first lines of paragraphs uniformly, about an inch in longhand and five spaces in typewritten copy. Leave no long gap at the end of any line except the last one in the paragraph. Use Arabic numerals in the upper right-hand corner to mark all pages after the first. Center the title on the page about an inch and a half from the top or on the first ruled line. Leave the next line blank and begin the first paragraph on the third line. In this way the title will be made to stand out from the text. Endorse the theme in the way designated by your instructor.

Legibility Make each word a distinct unit: join all the letters of a word and leave adequate space before beginning the next word. Shape each letter distinctly. Avoid flourishes. Many pages of manuscript generally artistic and attractive to the eye are almost illegible. Dot each *i*, not some other letter nearby. Cross each *t*, not an adjoining *h* or some other letter. Make dots and periods real dots, not small circles. Let all capitals stand out distinctly as capitals and keep all small letters down to the average height of other small letters. Remember that you will not be present to tell the reader which letters you intend to be capitals, which to be small letters.

Syllabication Never divide a word of a single syllable at the end of a line. Divide other words only between syllables (parts pronounced as separate units of a word). Do not confuse the reader by setting off an *-ed* pronounced as a part of the preceding syllable (as in *forced, opened, reared*). The simplest way to check syllabication is to refer to the word in the dictionary. For detailed rules regarding syllabication, consult an unabridged dictionary.

Revision of Your Written Work

You learn how to write chiefly by correcting your own errors. Corrections made for you are of comparatively little value. Therefore the instructor points out the errors but allows you to make the actual revision for yourself. The instructor usually indicates a necessary correction by a number (or a symbol) marked in the margin of the theme opposite the error. If a word is misspelled, the number **18** (or the symbol **sp**) will be used; if there is a sentence fragment, the number **2** (or the symbol **frag**); if there is a faulty reference of a pronoun, the number **28** (or the symbol **ref**). Consult the text (see the guides on the inside covers), master the principle underlying each correction, and make the necessary revisions in red. Draw one red line through words to be deleted, but allow such words to remain legible in order that the instructor may compare the revised form with the original.

The Comma After the number **12** in the margin you should take special care to supply the appropriate letter (**a, b, c,** or **d**) from the explanatory section on pages 55–62 to show why the comma is needed. The act of inserting a comma teaches little; understanding why it is required in a particular situation is a definite step toward mastery of the comma. (Your instructor may require that you pinpoint each of your own errors by supplying the appropriate letter after every number he writes in the margin.)

Specimen Paragraph from a Student Theme

Marked by the Instructor with Symbols

cs   Making photographs for newspapers is hard work, it is not

2/   the romantic carefree adventure glorified in motion pictures

       and fiction books. For every great moment recorded by the

sp   stareing eye of the camera, there are twenty routine assign-

ref   ments that must be handled in the same efficient manner. He

       must often overcome great hardships. The work continues for

sub   long hours. It must meet the deadline. At times he is called

       upon to risk his own life to secure a picture. To the news-

frag paper photographer, getting his picture being the most impor-

       tant thing.

3   Making photographs for newspapers is hard work, it is not

/2   the romantic carefree adventure glorified in motion pictures

and fiction books. For every great moment recorded by the

18   stareing eye of the camera, there are twenty routine assign-

28   ments that must be handled in the same efficient manner. He

must often overcome great hardships. The work continues for

24

long hours. It must meet the deadline. At times he is called

upon to risk his own life to secure a picture. To the news-

2   paper photographer, getting his picture being the most impor-

tant thing.

Corrected by the Student

3   Making photographs for newspapers is hard work, ;it is not

/2C the romantic, carefree adventure glorified in motion pictures

and fiction books. For every great moment recorded by the

        staring
18   ~~stareing~~ eye of the camera, there are twenty routine assign-

                                                        The
28   ments that must be handled in the same efficient manner. ~~He~~
newspaper photographer must often overcome great
~~must often overcome great hardships.~~ ~~The work continues~~ for
24 *hardships and work long hours to meet the deadline.*
~~long hours. It must meet the deadline.~~ At times he is called

upon to risk his own life to secure a picture. To the news-

                                                is
2   paper photographer, getting his picture ~~being~~ the most impor-

tant thing.

Sentence Sense

1

The first step in learning to write clearly and effectively is to understand the sentence.

1a Learn to recognize the verb, the nucleus of the sentence.

Without a verb no group of words is grammatically a sentence.

> a college student
> a college student with no shoes on
> A college student with no shoes on *rode* the motorcycle.

Only the third of these groups of words really makes a complete statement. The word *rode* is the vital word. Omit it, and the sentence becomes merely a fragment—not a sentence at all.

A verb may be recognized by its form and its meaning.

Form   When converted from present to past tense, nearly all verbs change form: *ride—rode, am—was, love—loved.* When converted from first person to third person singular, in the present tense, all verbs change form: *I ride—he rides, I am—he is, I love—he loves.* All verbs in the progressive tense end in *-ing: I am riding, I am being, I am loving.* Such form changes are called inflections (or conjugations).

Meaning   A verb may express action (He *rides* wildly), indicate a state of being (He *is* sick), assert something (He *loves* peace), make a statement (He *is riding*), ask a question (*Is* he *riding?*), or give a command (*Ride* now).

Verb phrases   A verb phrase (or cluster) is made up of a verb and one or more auxiliaries, or "helping verbs": *rides > is riding, has been riding, should have been riding.* Common auxiliaries are *am, is, are, was, were, be, been, has, have, had, do, does, did, may, might, must, shall, will, would, should, ought to, can,* and *could.*

The words that make up a verb phrase are often separated (He *did* not really *ride* the camel. *Could* he *have ridden* the camel?). Neither the adverb *not* nor its contraction (did*n't*) is ever a part of the verb.

Verbs and particles   Sometimes a particle like *with, up,* or *up with* accompanies the verb to make a single unit of meaning.

> Astronauts must *put up with* many inconveniences.
> They *put in* many months of grueling study and practice.

1b Learn to recognize subjects and objects of verbs.

Subjects In every grammatically complete sentence the verb has a subject. However, in a command or a request the subject is often implied rather than actually included in the sentence: Ride quickly (*You* ride quickly).

In a sentence that asks a question, the subject can be found more easily if the sentence is rephrased in the form of a statement:

> Did the *astronauts* reach the moon?
> The *astronauts* did reach the moon.

The complete subject is the subject and all words associated with it; likewise, the complete predicate is the verb along with associated words and phrases.

> *Complete Subject*   *Complete Predicate*
> El Greco, the Greek painter,   lived in Spain.

Objects Often the verb has an object—a word or group of words that receives, or is in some way affected by, the action of the verb.

> Thomas Jefferson wrote the *Declaration of Independence*.
> He also founded the *University of Virginia*.

Occasionally verbs such as *buy, bring, give, lend, offer, sell,* or *send* have not only a direct object but also an indirect object which states to whom or for whom something is done:

> You can't teach an old *dog* new tricks.
> He gave the *poor* food.

A few verbs, such as *is*, do not take objects, but complements which refer to the subject:

> Leonardo was a *painter*. [*Painter* is not the object of *was*, but refers to the subject *Leonardo*.]
> He also became an *inventor*. [*Inventor* refers to *He*.]

Tests for Subject and Object

In a sentence subjects and objects may be recognized by form, meaning, and position.

Form   Subjects and objects of verbs are either nouns or noun substitutes such as pronouns. The most commonly used pronouns have one form for the subject and a different form for the object: *I—me, he—him, she—her, they—them, who—whom*. Nearly all nouns (words used to name persons, places, things, ideas, or actions) change form to indicate number: *boy—boys, man—men, city—cities*. The articles *a, an,* and *the* are sometimes called "noun determiners" or "noun indicators," because they regularly point to a following noun: a *boy*, an *apple*, the big *apple*.

Meaning   To find the subject, simply ask in connection with the verb, "Who or what?"

The father bought his children expensive presents.

"Who bought? The *father* bought." *Father* is thus shown to be the subject.

To find the object, ask "Whom or what?" received the action or effect of the verb. "The father bought what? The father bought *presents*." So *presents* is proved to be the object. Another characteristic of the object is that it can be made the subject of the passive form of the verb. "*Presents* were bought by the father."

The indirect object is shown by asking "To whom or for whom?" (or "To what or for what?") something is done: "For whom did the father buy presents? The father bought presents for his *children*." Thus *children* is shown to be the indirect object.

Position   A third way to recognize subjects and objects is to become thoroughly familiar with the usual word order of English sentences. This is usually subject—verb—object. Observe the importance of word order in determining meaning.

PATTERN 1   SUBJECT—VERB.

The campus *newspaper is published* daily.
Opinions about campus violence *vary*.

PATTERN 2   SUBJECT—VERB—OBJECT.

Newspapers have different editorial *outlooks*.
One should read several *newspapers*.

PATTERN 3   SUBJECT—VERB—INDIRECT OBJECT—DIRECT OBJECT.

The *judges presented* the winning relay *team* its *trophy*.
The *team showed us* a fine *example* of baton-handling.

For patterns with subject complements, see **4b**.

The preceding three sentence patterns may be varied in several ways, primarily by the use of *there* (an expletive or introductory word) and by a shift to interrogative (question) word order. Notice that the order of the sentence parts changes with such variation.

There was a new bowl added this year.   [Variation of Pattern 1]
What do you think about astrology?   [Variation of Pattern 2]
Did the director give his actors believable stage movements?   [Variation of Pattern 3]

Compounds   Subjects, verbs, and objects may be compound.

Michelangelo and *Leonardo* were famous artists.
Michelangelo *painted* and *sculpted.*
Leonardo produced both *art* and various *inventions*.

1c   Learn to recognize all the parts of speech.

Words are usually grouped into eight word classes, or "parts of speech," according to their uses in the sentence.

Parts of Speech	Uses in the Sentence	Examples
1. Verbs	Indicators of action or state of being (often link subjects and complements)	Tom *hit* the curve. Mary *was* tired. He *is* a senator.
2. Nouns	Subjects, objects, complements	*Kay* gave *Ron* the *book* of *poems*.
3. Pronouns	Substitutes for nouns	*He* will return *it* to *her* later.
4. Adjectives	Modifiers of nouns and noun substitutes	*The long* poem is *the best*.
5. Adverbs	Modifiers of verbs, adjectives, adverbs, or whole clauses	sang *loudly* a *very* sad song *entirely too* fast
6. Prepositions	Words used before nouns and noun substitutes to relate them to other words in the sentence	*to* the lake *in* a hurry *with* no thought
7. Conjunctions	Connectives	win *or* lose good *but* dull Come *as* you are.
8. Interjections	Expressions of emotion (unrelated grammatically to the rest of the sentence)	*Woe* is me! *Ouch!* *Imagine!*

The dictionary lists the word class or classes in which a given word may be used, but the actual classification of a word depends on its use in a sentence.

1d   Learn to recognize phrases and subordinate clauses.

PHRASES

A phrase is a group of related words, without both a subject and a predicate, that is used as a noun, a verb, or a modifier (adjective or adverb).

NOUN PHRASE   *To read* is *to discover truth*.   [The noun phrases act as subject and complement.]

VERB PHRASE   He *has read* all the novels of Dostoevski.

MODIFYING PHRASE   The English novel *as a genre* made its appearance *during the eighteenth century*.   [The first modifying phrase is an adjective; the second, an adverb.]

Phrases may also be classified as prepositional phrases or verbal phrases.

Prepositional phrases   The prepositional phrase is a related word group that begins with a preposition and concludes with a noun called the object of the preposition. Prepositional phrases normally function as modifiers, and they often occur in groups.

> The girl *with no date for the dance* sat *in her dormitory room.*   [*With no date* modifies *girl; for the dance* modifies *date;* and *in her dormitory room* modifies *sat.*]

Verbal phrases   A phrase introduced by a participle, a gerund, or an infinitive is called a verbal phrase. Participles, gerunds, and infinitives are derived from verbs and are much like verbs in that they have different tenses, can have subjects and objects, and can be modified by adverbs. But they are not true verbs; they cannot function as the only verb form in the sentence.

> VERB   The girl *made* an Indian headband.
>
> VERBAL   The girl *making* an Indian headband has lived on a reservation. [The verbal *making* requires another verb form in the sentence— *has lived.*]

Verbal phrases—participial, gerund, and infinitive—function as nouns or modifiers in sentences.

> PARTICIPIAL PHRASE   The students *wearing the orange and white caps* are freshmen.   [The participial phrase functions as an adjective modifying students.]
>
> GERUND PHRASE   *Learning a second language* requires perseverance.   [The gerund phrase functions as a noun, the subject of the sentence.]
>
> INFINITIVE PHRASE   The one thing *never to forget* is *to hold your head high.* [The first infinitive phrase functions as an adjective modifying *thing;* the second functions as a noun, the complement of the verb *is.*]

Notice that both the present participle and the gerund end in -*ing* and that they can be distinguished only by their use in the sentence: the participle is an adjective and the gerund is a noun.

Infinitive phrases are made up of *to* plus the verb form and may function as either nouns or modifiers.

CLAUSES

A clause is a group of related words containing a verb and its subject. If a clause can stand alone as a simple sentence, it is called a main (or independent) clause; if it cannot, it is called a subordinate (or dependent) clause.

> The students waited *while the speaker searched for the chalk.*   [Main clause followed by a subordinate clause]

If these clauses are separated, we have a simple sentence and a sentence fragment.

The students waited.   [Simple sentence]
While the speaker searched for the chalk.   [Sentence fragment]

The subordinating conjunction *while* makes the clause that follows it subordinate. (Some other words that frequently introduce subordinate clauses are *when, if, since, because, although, whoever, who, which,* and *that.*)

Subordinate clauses may function in sentences either as modifiers (adjectives or adverbs) or as nouns.

Adverb clauses   Adverb clauses frequently modify verbs, but they may also modify adjectives, adverbs, verbals, prepositional phrases, or even main clauses. An adverb clause, like an individual adverb, may be placed at various positions in the sentence.

> *When the dog was found,* everyone sighed with relief.   [A comma usually follows an introductory adverb clause.]
> Everyone sighed with relief *when the dog was found.*   [Usually no comma is used with a concluding adverb clause.]

Adjective clauses   Adjective clauses, which are normally introduced by a relative pronoun like *who, which,* or *that,* are usually located immediately after the nouns or pronouns they modify.

> The dog, *which we finally found,* was unharmed.

Sometimes the relative pronoun is omitted if the adjective clause is short.

> The speaker (*whom*) *we wanted* was not available.   [The relative pronoun is understood but not stated in the sentence.]

Noun clauses   Noun clauses have the same functions that nouns have.

> *Whoever would speak on short notice* was invited.   [The noun clause is used as the subject of the verb.]

1e   Learn to recognize various types of sentences.

Sentences may be classified structurally as simple, compound, complex, or compound-complex. A simple sentence is made up of one main clause.

> The Borghese Gardens are free to the public.

A compound sentence is made up of two or more main clauses.

> The Borghese Gardens are free to the public, and many Romans visit them.

A complex sentence is made up of one main clause and at least one subordinate clause.

> The Borghese Gardens, which are two miles square, are free to the public.

A compound-complex sentence is made up of two or more main clauses and at least one subordinate clause.

> The Borghese Gardens, which are two miles square, are free to the public, and many Romans visit them.

NAME _____ SCORE _____

DIRECTIONS   In the following sentences underline the subject once, the verb twice, and the direct object of the verb (if any) three times. Then enter all three in the blanks below the sentences, noting that the subject and verb always agree in number.

EXAMPLE	*Subject*	*Verb*	*Object*

We hear a great deal about the battle of the sexes.
＿＿ ＝＝ 　　　＝＝　　 *We* 　　 *hear* 　　 *deal*

1. Much has been written about the eternal struggle between the sexes.

   _____   _____   _____

2. For many centuries the male was traditionally considered the superior sex.

   _____   _____   _____

3. Even today this opinion still exists among some men.

   _____   _____   _____

4. This particular attitude is called male chauvinism.

   _____   _____   _____

5. Perhaps women have always questioned the chauvinistic view.

   _____   _____   _____

6. But in the last few years there has appeared a united movement against male chauvinism.

   _____   _____   _____

7. The women's liberation movement has gained increasing support since the 1960's.

   _____   _____   _____

8. This movement is often called the feminist movement.

   _____   _____   _____

9. Feminism is, of course, seriously opposed to male chauvinism.

   _____   _____   _____

10. The feminists register many complaints against the male's attitude toward the female.

   _____   _____   _____

11. How many of their complaints do you know? 　　 *do know* 　 *many complaints*
   _____ *you* _____   _____   _____

	Subject	Verb	Object

12. Which **one receives** the most **attention** from the feminists?

_____   _____   _____

13. Among the many complaints **one** particularly **stands** out.

_____   _____   _____

14. **Men give** women **credit** for little except their attractiveness.

_____   _____   _____

15. **They see women** as Miss America contestants, as *Playboy* centerfolds, and as pretty, stay-at-home housewives.

_____   _____   _____

16. This **attitude** toward woman **eliminates** any recognition of her **ability to compete** mentally with man.

_____   _____   *recognition*

17. **Male chauvinists** quite naturally **present** a different **picture** of themselves.

_____   _____   _____

18. **They see** no **harm** in exalting woman's beauty.

_____   _____   _____

19. **Women possess** a different type of **intelligence** from men.

_____   _____   *Type*

20. **Women's** particular intellectual **gifts qualify** them uniquely for the **roles** of homemakers and mothers.

_____   _____   *Them*

Assignment 9 Feb 74

Subject and verb in compound sentences Exercise 1-2

NAME _____ SCORE _____

DIRECTIONS   Insert an inverted caret (V) between main clauses in the following compound sentences. Then enter in the blanks at the right the subject and verb of each main clause. Note that the clauses are correctly joined either (1) by a comma plus *and, but, or, nor,* or *for,* or (2) by a semicolon.

EXAMPLE	*Subject*	*Verb*
There are many interesting studies of the male and female roles in courtship;ᵛ one among them is Albert Ellis's *The American Sexual Tragedy.*	*studies*	*are*
	one	*is*

1. Albert Ellis sees many of the difficulties between the sexes as resulting from the modern tradition of romantic love; this tradition fosters illusions about the nature of love.

2. The female, according to Ellis, uses the "Sex Tease" game; that is, she uses sex to conquer the male.

3. She uses her physical beauty to attract the male; but she must not readily give in to his advances toward her.

4. She must use the "Sex Tease" to achieve her goal; and her goal is, of course, marriage.

5. The "Sex Tease" pattern came in with the romantic movement; and it has shaped male-female relationships ever since.

6. Romantic love is actually a relatively modern development; it originated as a protest against rigid patterns of twelfth-century life.

7. At first it opposed the established so-
   cial order; it emphasized human love
   rather than divine love.

8. It often defied marriage, for the
   lovers were free to love and then to
   part.

9. Eventually, though, romantic love
   took on many of the trappings of the
   Christian version of love; it became,
   according to Ellis, antisexual.

10. The sensual was (condemned) and
    chasteness was (glorified.)

11. Medieval romanticism was different
    from modern romanticism, however,
    for it had little to do with marriage.

12. Sexual desire and love were not con-
    sidered the same; thus a troubadour
    might well love many women with-
    out wanting to marry any of them.

13. Love and marriage did not go to-
    gether "like a horse and carriage";
    indeed, throughout most of man's
    history romantic love has been con-
    sidered a special kind of madness.

14. One might become romantically in-
    volved with someone he desired,
    but he would not necessarily marry
    her as a result of his temporary mad-
    ness.

15. Today romantic love and marriage
    have become synonymous; and, ac-
    cording to Ellis and many other psy-
    chologists, the merging of the two
    has had disastrous effects on male-
    female relationships.

Subordinate (dependent) clauses

NAME _____ SCORE _____

DIRECTIONS   Bracket the subordinate clauses in the following sentences. Then in the blanks at the right classify each clause as an adjective (*adj*), an adverb (*adv*), or a noun (*n*) and write out the first word of the clause. If you need further practice in identifying subjects and verbs, underline each subject once and each verb twice.

EXAMPLE

Clause

Ashley Montagu, a famous English anthropologist, contends [that women are superior to men.]

n   *that*

1. According to Ashley Montagu, we have finally arrived at the time when women are no longer subservient to men.

2. For centuries it was believed that women were inferior in intelligence to men.

3. A woman, who by nature was given to emotional instability and physical weakness, was thought capable of performing only routine tasks.

4. World War I, when women had to replace men in various occupations, did much to alter the old attitudes toward woman's place.

5. By the end of the war it was generally agreed that women performed jobs outside the home quite well.

6. Positions which formerly had been closed to them now began to open.

7. During World War II employers were more than willing to accept women workers, especially in fields where delicate precision work was required.

8. Although woman has made progress toward her liberation, she still has far to go.

9. She has, according to Montagu, freed herself from thralldom to man but not from the myth that she is inferior to man.

   _____   _____

10. One may well ask what evidence Montagu offers for the superiority of the female.

    _____   _____

11. He begins with the argument that woman's chromosomal structure is superior to man's.

    _____   _____

12. In fact, Montagu suggests that the structure of chromosomes in the male is incomplete.

    _____   _____

13. When a male is formed, he is no more than an incomplete female because of his chromosomal deficiency.

    _____   _____

14. Because he is deficient in X chromosomes, the male cannot produce children.

    _____   _____

15. This incapacity deprives him from developing the close parent-child relationship which the mother achieves.

    _____   _____

16. Since the parent-child relationship is the model for all human relationships, the female has always been the more humane sex.

    _____   _____

17. The female possesses a far greater understanding of human nature than the male does.

    _____   _____

18. Unlike the male, who is by nature aggressive, the female is naturally inclined to be loving.

    _____   _____

19. Thus it is woman's duty to teach man what it means to be human.

    _____   _____

20. As Montagu sees it, woman's peculiar genius for being human has been too long undervalued.

    _____   _____

NAME _____ SCORE _____

DIRECTIONS   In the following sentences classify each italicized phrase as a noun (*n*), a verb (*v*), or a modifier (*mod*). Remember that a phrase used as a modifier may function as either an adjective or an adverb. (You may want to practice identifying the noun and modifying phrases as prepositional phrases, infinitive phrases, participial phrases, or gerund phrases.)

		Phrase
EXAMPLE		
Arguing against Montagu, Lester David asserts that women are inferior to men.		*mod*

1. Lester David recognizes all the traditional claims *about woman's mental inferiority.*   _____

2. *In addition,* he claims she is inferior in character to the male.   _____

3. It is woman's nature *to be obstinate, suspicious, and even unethical.*   _____

4. Lester David relies on examples *to prove his thesis.*   _____

5. *Looking at the number* of women's names in an encyclopedia gives an indication of woman's place in history.   _____

6. A search of the encyclopedia *will produce* fewer than one thousand names, David claims.   _____

7. David concludes that few women have accomplished anything of significance in any *of the creative fields.*   _____

8. *To explain her lack* of accomplishment is impossible except in terms of her lack of ability.   _____

9. *Countering the argument* that men have had more opportunities than women, David points out that genius always makes its own opportunity.   _____

10. Most of the geniuses *recorded in history* have had to work against great odds to succeed.   _____

11. It *has* long *been supposed* that woman is superior in constitution to man, but David cites evidence otherwise.   _____

12. While women do live longer than men, they are much more susceptible *to illness,* whether physical or mental, than are men.   _____

13. *Until now* it has been assumed that women are superior in the handling of children.   _____

14. But David, while recognizing that women may be more skill-
    ful in feeding and clothing babies, argues that men are supe-
    rior to women *in the general supervision* of children.   _____

15. David manages *to dismiss the greater number* of male crimi-
    nal convictions by claiming that the legal system favors the
    female.   _____

16. Besides, he argues that women *are* basically *given* to lying, a
    definite character deficiency.   _____

17. David disagrees with Ashley Montagu's thesis that men are
    envious of women's ability *to bear children.*   _____

18. He claims that women are envious of men, as evidenced by
    their penchant *for wearing men's clothing.*   _____

19. David notes that no normal male would don female attire for
    anything *except a gag.*   _____

20. *On the other hand,* women typically wear long pants, sweat
    shirts, and other male garments.   _____

NAME _____ SCORE _____

DIRECTIONS   Classify the following sentences as simple (*S*), compound (*CD*), complex (*CX*), or compound-complex (*CC*).

Type of Sentence

EXAMPLE

For many years Betty Friedan has been an important spokesman for women's rights.   *S*

1. Betty Friedan's book *The Feminine Mystique,* which appeared in 1963, is required reading for anyone interested in the women's liberation movement.   _____

2. In her book Miss Friedan explores woman's role in the modern world.   _____

3. It is her contention that women today suffer an identity crisis; that is, modern women do not know what their role in life is.   _____

4. Many have rejected the kind of life their mothers knew, but they have not found a new life of their own.   _____

5. Too often their image of what they should be is molded by advertising.   _____

6. In an effort to avoid the limited role in life of their mothers, some girls seek only popularity; consequently, they limit themselves by a different kind of stereotype.   _____

7. Betty Friedan interviewed many high school girls who had showed intellectual promise but who had abruptly ended their education.   _____

8. These girls had concluded that they must imitate in every respect the qualities of the popular girl, and they quickly determined that academic achievement was not one of these qualities.   _____

9. Because these girls feared becoming like their mothers, they refused to grow up; they denied developing their best qualities in order to fit the stereotype of the popular girl.   _____

10. Betty Friedan argues that every woman must face an identity crisis, just as every man must.   _____

11. Men must usually determine who they are and where they are headed by the time they finish college, or at least by

their early thirties; but women can prolong the confrontation until their forties.   _____

12. They may escape coming to grips with their identity by marrying early and having many children.   _____

13. Eventually, though, the role of motherhood ends, and they must find a new role.   _____

14. For many centuries few women married and had children and also pursued careers.   _____

15. The typical old maid with a career was a woman few envied.   _____

16. But today new careers are open to women, and greater freedom permits women to have both families and careers.   _____

17. Thus the young college woman of today must face the same identity crisis that the young man faces.   _____

18. She can no longer satisfy her need for achievement by assuming the identity of her husband.   _____

19. If she does expect to achieve her total fulfillment through marriage, she is succumbing to the feminine mystique.   _____

20. At one age or another she will discover that the feminine mystique is an illusion, that her identity cannot be determined solely by her biological make-up.   _____

Sentence Fragment frag 2

2

Do not carelessly write an ineffective sentence fragment—a phrase or a subordinate clause—as if it were a complete sentence.

People frequently use sentence fragments effectively in speech and sometimes in writing. Any telephone conversation clearly illustrates the use of sentence fragments that communicate the speaker's thoughts. Generally, though, in formal speeches and writing, complete sentences are used.

A sentence fragment is usually either a phrase or a subordinate clause detached from a main clause. To be complete, a sentence must contain at least one main clause. A sentence fragment may be corrected (1) by making it into a sentence or (2) by attaching it to a sentence or to a main clause.

> PHRASE   Having only one tusk.   [Participial phrase]
>
> SENTENCE   The elephant had only one tusk.   [Fragment made into a sentence]
>
> SENTENCE   Having only one tusk, the elephant lost the fight.   [Fragment attached to a main clause]
>
> SUBORDINATE CLAUSE   Because the elephant had only one tusk.   [Subordinate clause]
>
> SENTENCE   The elephant had only one tusk.   [Fragment made into a sentence]
>
> SENTENCE   Because the elephant had only one tusk, he lost the fight.   [Fragment attached to a main clause]

As you proofread your compositions, check for sentence fragments by asking yourself two questions: (1) Does each word group that is punctuated as a sentence have both a subject and a predicate? (2) If a clause is introduced by a subordinator or a relative pronoun, is a main or independent clause also included in the word group?

Comma Splice and Fused Sentence cs 3

3

Do not carelessly link two main clauses (sentences) with only a comma between them (comma splice) or run main clauses together without any punctuation (fused sentence).

> COMMA SPLICE   The newly married couple needed to save money, they built their own beach house.   [Two main clauses linked by only a comma]

17

FUSED SENTENCE	The newly married couple needed to save money they built their own beach house. [Two main clauses run together with no punctuation]

Often the best way to correct the comma splice or fused sentence is to subordinate one of the main clauses.

REVISION 1	Because the newly married couple needed to save money, they built their own beach house.
PATTERN	SUBORDINATE CLAUSE, MAIN CLAUSE.

The subordinate clause, of course, may follow the main clause, in which case there is usually no need for the comma.

	The newly married couple built their own beach house because they needed to save money.
PATTERN	MAIN CLAUSE SUBORDINATE CLAUSE.

There are several other methods of correction.

REVISION 2	The newly married couple needed to save money. They built their own beach house.
PATTERN	SENTENCE. SENTENCE.
REVISION 3	The newly married couple had little money, but they wanted their own beach house.
PATTERN	MAIN CLAUSE, coordinating conjunction MAIN CLAUSE.
REVISION 4	The newly married couple needed to save money; they built their own beach house.
PATTERN	MAIN CLAUSE; MAIN CLAUSE.

Caution: Whenever a conjunctive adverb (such as *however, therefore*), a transitional phrase (such as *for example, in fact*), or a direct quotation is used, one must be especially careful to avoid the comma splice or fused sentence.

COMMA SPLICE	The newly married couple needed to save money, therefore they built their own beach house.
REVISED	The newly married couple needed to save money; therefore they built their own beach house.
FUSED SENTENCE	The newly married couple showed their versatility in many ways for example they built their own beach house.
REVISED	The newly married couple showed their versatility in many ways; for example, they built their own beach house.
COMMA SPLICE	"Many people have lost the ability to do things with their hands," the couple said, "we want to preserve that ability."
REVISED	"Many people have lost the ability to do things with their hands," the couple said. "We want to preserve that ability."

While comma splices and fused sentences sometimes appear in fiction and even in essays, the inexperienced writer will do well to make sure that main clauses in a sentence are separated (1) by a comma plus a coordinating conjunction or (2) by a semicolon.

NAME _____ SCORE _____

DIRECTIONS   In the following word groups underline each subject with one straight line, each verbal with one wavy line, and each verb with two straight lines. Then enter the subject and verb of each sentence in the blanks at the right. If a word group contains no true subject and verb, indicate a sentence fragment by writing *frag* in the blank for the verb. Some fragments have neither subjects nor verbs.

EXAMPLE   *Subject*   *Verb*

An interesting analysis of masculinity written   *analysis*   *frag*
    by Lee R. Steiner.

1. Lee Steiner discussing the identity crisis
   of man.   _____   _____

2. Men are tired of their role.   _____   _____

3. The impossibility of fulfilling the stereo-
   type of masculinity.   _____   _____

4. Television and movies having popularized
   the notion of the swaggering frontiers-
   man.   _____   _____

5. A real man must be strong and smart
   and an ardent lover.   _____   _____

6. Early in life a boy becomes confused
   about his role.   _____   _____

7. Many of the qualities expected of him are
   indeed contradictory.   _____   _____

8. As a child being obedient to his mother
   but aggressive with his peers.   _____   _____

9. In school he is expected to be superior to
   his female classmates.   _____   _____

10. Yet many of the girls can outstrip him in
    intellectual achievement.   _____   _____

11. Courtship being perhaps the most confus-
    ing time of all.   _____   _____

12. The man having been given the role of
    the pursuer.   _____   _____

		Subject	Verb

13. But, in reality, he is the pursued.

14. Every girl knowing how to pursue her man while seeming to be pursued by him.

15. Once married, he is supposed to be the wage earner and the strong protector.

16. Not failing, however, to be gentle and kind as well.

17. And at work he must exhibit aggressiveness in his attempts to advance but, at the same time, considerateness in his attitude toward his fellow workers.

18. No wonder modern man is frustrated.

19. He can never meet all of the qualifications for masculinity imposed upon him.

20. Eliminating the stereotype of masculinity would give a man some hope of being recognized for his own individual qualities of manhood.

NAME _____ SCORE _____

DIRECTIONS   The following word groups show that a sentence fragment is often placed before or after a closely related complete thought. First identify each complete sentence by writing C in the numbered blank at the right, and each fragment by writing *frag*. Then complete each fragment (1) by rewriting it to form a sentence by itself or (2) by attaching the fragment to the complete sentence. If you consider some other method of correction preferable, be prepared to point it out.

EXAMPLES

¹ Apparently men as well as women are struggling to free   1.___*C*___

themselves from stereotyped images. ² Their struggle ~~being~~   2.___*frag*___
                                                    is^

manifest in several ways.

¹The 1960's and 1970's have seen many changes in pat-   1._____

terns of behavior and dress for men and women. ²Some   2._____

people claim they can hardly tell the difference between

men and women any more. ³Since many men wear their   3._____

hair long and many women dress in what once was con-

sidered men's clothing. ⁴Many a man has stopped to pick   4._____

up a female hitchhiker. ⁵Only to discover that the girl is a   5._____

boy with shoulder-length hair. ⁶On the other hand, what   6._____

may seem to be a male hitchhiker turning out to be a girl

in dungarees and a long, loose shirt. ⁷This change in the   7._____

dress code being but one way that many men and women

have shown their rejection of the stereotyped male and fe-

male roles.

⁸Some of the other manifestations of this rejection are   8._____

even more dramatic. ⁹Such as the "burn the bra" movement   9._____

among feminists. ¹⁰Seeking still further release from the   10._____

housewife image. ¹¹The feminists have urged the adoption   11._____

of "Ms." as the title for both married and single women.

¹²They ask, "If men do not have to change their title from   12._____

'Mr.' to something else when they marry. ¹³Why should
women have to make the switch from 'Miss' to 'Mrs.'?" ¹⁴In
1972 women got their first nude male centerfold. ¹⁵An obvious parallel to the nude female centerfolds in *Playboy*
and other male magazines.

¹⁶Although the woman's rejection of her stereotyped
image has been more frequently discussed than the man's
rejection of his set role. ¹⁷There still have been many news-
worthy efforts by men. ¹⁸For example, the attempt by one
man to legally marry another man and make him his heir.
¹⁹Far more common, many men now assuming the role of
housewife. ²⁰They stay home with the children and do the
cleaning and cooking. ²¹While the wives become the bread-
winners for the family. ²²There is also a popular movement
among men to participate actively in the birth process.
²³Which was formerly witnessed only by the mother and
her medical attendants.

²⁴All of these variations from the traditional male and
female roles show that there is indeed a sexual revolution.
²⁵And it may only be beginning.

13._____

14._____

15._____

16._____

17._____

18._____

19._____

20._____

21._____

22._____

23._____

24._____

25._____

NAME _____ SCORE _____

DIRECTIONS   In each of the following sentences insert an inverted caret (V) between main clauses where a comma splice might occur. Then indicate in the first blank at the right whether the sentence is correct (C), contains a comma splice (CS), or is fused (F). Correct each error by the best method, showing in the second blank whether you have used subordination (sub), a period (.), a semicolon (;), or a comma plus a coordinating conjunction (conj).

EXAMPLES

There is a movement among men to become more attractive; it is often referred to as the "peacock revolution."   _F_ _;_

The peacock revolution reminds one of the women's liberation movement, ~~the women's movement~~ which may indeed have given it birth.   _CS_ _sub_

1. Women are seeking to compete professionally with men thus men must seek to compete sexually with women.   _____ _____

2. Women have invaded the job market, men, according to many sociologists, must invade the sex market.   _____ _____

3. The efforts of men to beautify themselves may be traced far back in time, they may be traced as far back as prehistoric times.   _____ _____

4. Primitive men sought to improve their looks, they applied cosmetics made from roots, berries, and nuts.   _____ _____

5. There were other early attempts at beautification, for example, men used feathers and skins to adorn their bodies.   _____ _____

6. Egyptian men used perfumed oils in their baths and ointments on their hair they used these beauty aids as early as 3000 B.C.   _____ _____

7. Greek and Roman men lightened their skin with chalk, Babylonian men chose to darken their skin by applying rouge. _____ _____

8. Courtly men during the sixteenth century made great use of color, the French painted the veins in their temples blue and the English dyed their beards orange. _____ _____

9. And perfume was used extravagantly by all European men, the perfume was a substitute for the daily bath, which people frowned upon for many centuries. _____ _____

10. Thus the male effort to be beautiful did not originate with Beau Brummel, it is not likely to die out with the best dressed men of the 1970's. _____ _____

11. Male beautification, then, is not a fad, as much as some critics of the age may wish that it were. _____ _____

12. The modern interest in male sex appeal may have resulted from Elvis Presley's gyrations during the 1950's, Elvis was, in effect, male cheesecake. _____ _____

13. Whatever the cause of modern man's desire to be beautiful, it is obviously a lasting desire. _____ _____

14. Advertising is careful to use the term *grooming aids*, hair spray and aftershave lotions and colognes are still cosmetics. _____ _____

15. The male cosmetic industry has boomed, in fact, its growth has been about 50 percent greater than the female's during the 1960's. _____ _____

16. Modern men have more leisure time and more money, consequently, they are turning to cosmetics and flamboyant hair styles and dress. _____ _____

NAME _____ SCORE _____

17. Men are seeking to prolong their attractiveness through the use of many techniques, some of them quite expensive, they try girdles, hair transplants, and face lifts. _____ _____

18. Men, like women, want to be attractive, they will try almost anything to make themselves so, even charm schools. _____ _____

19. Men's styles may change during the next few years, men's concern with attractiveness probably will not. _____ _____

20. Men may decide to shave their heads rather than wear long hair, however, they will still be seeking what they think is an attractive appearance. _____ _____

21. Some men have already shown their acceptance of high-heeled shoes and shoulder bags, once considered appropriate only for women. _____ _____

22. Perhaps male cosmetics will one day include lipstick and eye shadow then cosmetic companies might call on men at work. _____ _____

23. Of course, many, if not most, men do not accept what they consider extreme dress, even the most conservative men now wear clothes that they would have scorned a few years ago. _____ _____

24. The stereotype of what is masculine in appearance seems on the way out, if it has not already gone. _____ _____

25. The peacock revolution and the women's liberation movement have caused men and women to reexamine their roles in society equally important, they have necessitated a reevaluation of male-female relationships. _____ _____

DIRECTIONS   Classify each of the following as a fragmentary sentence (*frag*), a comma splice (*CS*), or a correct sentence (*C*). Revise each faulty sentence.

EXAMPLE

One of the oldest debates of all ~~concerning~~ *concerns* the basic differences
between men and women.   *frag*

1. "Are there any basic differences between the sexes other than the biological ones?" one may well ask.   _____

2. The old stereotypes of male and female are breaking down, the question becomes even more difficult to answer.   _____

3. Some anthropologists, like Ashley Montagu, insist that there are psychological differences between men and women, these differences resulting from biological make-up.   _____

4. Other anthropologists hold that behavioral differences are almost entirely determined by environment, in other words, men act differently from women only because they have been conditioned by society to do so.   _____

5. Little girls are given dolls and playhouses and little boys are given guns and fire trucks, therein lies the cause for female domestication and male aggressiveness.   _____

6. If boys were conditioned to stay home and take care of the house and the children, they would be as gentle as little girls.   _____

7. Little girls, on the other hand, being conditioned to be as competitive as little boys.   _____

8. Some people argue that women are instinctively vain, while men are not.   _____

9. Women, too, have traditionally been regarded as fickle, are not the personifications of chance and fortune usually feminine?   _____

10. The female often having been labeled sneaky or under-handed in her dealings. _____

11. While those who have analyzed the male's character as aggressive by nature, inclined to compete and to fight. _____

12. The male is also typically regarded as direct or straightforward in his actions, not inclined to subtleties or deceptions. _____

13. "What do scientific studies show?" you ask, "are any differences in male and female behavior seen in very small infants?" _____

14. Even newborn male and female babies do show different reactions to stimuli. _____

15. For example, twelve-week-old female babies staring longer at photographs of faces than they do at geometric figures. _____

16. Male babies at this age stare at both equally, though later on they will show a preference for geometric figures. _____

17. Many scientists use this data to argue that women have a greater sensitivity to people than do men, thus women derive greater satisfaction from their relationships with people. _____

18. Then there are differences in the shapes of building blocks that boys and girls choose to play with. _____

19. And also in types of early intellectual development. _____

20. Boys handle mathematical and spatial reasoning better than girls do, but girls learn to count and to talk sooner than boys do. _____

4

Distinguish between adjectives and adverbs and use the appropriate forms.

Adjectives (in *italics* below) and adverbs (in **boldface** below) are modifiers. That is, they qualify or limit, make clearer or more specific, other words in the sentence. Any word modifying a noun or noun substitute is an adjective: *rapid* stream, *joyful* ringing of the bells. Any word modifying a verb, a participle, an infinitive, an adjective, another adverb, or even a whole clause is an adverb: flow **rapidly;** a **rapidly** *flowing* stream; a **very rapidly** *flowing* stream; **indeed,** the stream flows **rapidly.**

Forms of Adjectives and Adverbs

Both adjectives and adverbs usually have comparative forms: quick, quick*er,* quick*est;* quickly, **more** quickly, **most** quickly.

The *-ly* suffix nearly always makes adjectives into adverbs (*rapid,* **rapidly;** *joyful,* **joyfully**) and usually converts nouns into adjectives (friend, *friendly;* saint, *saintly*). Other suffixes that commonly make nouns into adjectives are *-al* (nation, *national*), *-ful* (hope, *hopeful*), *-ish* (boy, *boyish*), *-like* (life, *lifelike*), and *-ous* (danger, *dangerous*).

A few words ending in *-ly* (such as *only, early, cowardly*) may be either adjectives or adverbs, and the same is true for a considerable number of common words not ending in *-ly* (such as *far,* **far;** *fast,* **fast;** *late,* **late;** *little,* **little**).

Your dictionary shows the proper form for adjective and adverb, but you can know which form is needed only by determining the word modified.

4a   Use adverb forms as modifiers of verbs, adjectives, and other adverbs.

Especially common is the misuse of the adjective to modify a verb or verbal.

NONSTANDARD   Can one love as easy as one can hate?   [Adjective *easy* misused as a modifier of the verb *can love*]

STANDARD   Can one love as **easily** as one can hate?

NONSTANDARD   My mother sure makes good pizza.   [*Sure* misused as a modifier of *makes*]

STANDARD   My mother **surely** makes good pizza.

Another frequent error is the misuse of an adjective to modify another adjective.

NONSTANDARD   An accountant makes a real good salary.   [Adjective *real* misused as a modifier of the other adjective *good*]

STANDARD	An accountant makes a **really** good salary.
NONSTANDARD	This is a relative untapped market. [*Relative* misused as a modifier of *untapped*]
STANDARD	This is a **relatively** untapped market.

4b   Use adjectives rather than adverbs as subject complements.

As subject complements, adjectives always modify the subject. They usually follow but sometimes precede the verbs that link them with their subjects: *be, am, are, is, was, were, been, seen,* and *become* (and their equivalents) and *feel, taste, look, smell,* and *sound.*

PATTERN   SUBJECT—LINKING VERB—SUBJECT COMPLEMENT.
The rose smells *sweet.*   [*Sweet* rose]
Soft are the rose's petals.   [*Soft* petals]

Exception: The modifier should be an adverb when it refers to the action of the verb. In such a case the verb is not used as a linking verb.

PATTERN   SUBJECT—VERB—ADVERB.
The archeologist looked **expectantly** at the cave drawings. [The adverb **expectantly** qualifies the verb *looked.*]
The chef **suspiciously** tasted the strange mixture. [**Suspiciously** qualifies *tasted.*]

Note: A modifier following a verb and its direct object is an adjective when it refers to the object rather than to the action of the verb.

PATTERN   SUBJECT—VERB—OBJECT—OBJECT COMPLEMENT.
The engineer made the boiler *airtight.* [*Airtight* is an adjective: *airtight* boiler.]
The boy held his shoulders *straight.*   [*Straight* shoulders]

4c   Use appropriate forms for the comparative and the superlative.

| COMPARATIVE | Sophocles was the *better* of the two playwrights. [Used to compare two things: the suffix -*er* or the adverb **more,** as in *more beautiful,* is the usual sign of the comparative.] |
| SUPERLATIVE | Today Sophocles is the *most famous* of the Greek playwrights. [Commonly used to compare three or more things: the suffix -*est,* as in *wisest,* or the adverb **most** is the usual sign of the superlative.] |

4d   Avoid any awkward or ambiguous use of a noun form as an adjective.

Although many noun forms (*house* trailer, *boat* dock, *television* show) are used effectively as adjectives, especially when appropriate adjectives are not available, such forms should be avoided when they are either awkward or ambiguous.

| AWKWARD | Education methods are changing. |
| BETTER | *Educational* methods are changing. |

Confusion of adjectives and adverbs

Exercise 4-1

NAME _____ SCORE _____

DIRECTIONS   In each of the following sentences underline the word modified by the italicized word (or words) and indicate in the first blank at the right whether the italicized word (or words) is used as an adjective (*adj*) or an adverb (*adv*). In the second blank write *C* if the italicized word (or words) is the correct form for standard English; if not, supply the correct form.

EXAMPLES

Young boys and girls do <u>act</u> *different* when
    placed in similar situations.   *adv*   *differently*

<u>Boys</u> usually become *aggressive* in an un-
    pleasant situation whereas girls become
    passive.   *adj*   *C*

1. Boys seem more *independently* than girls
   at an early age.   _____   _____

2. For example, boys who are separated from
   their mothers by a barrier try *real* hard to
   knock it down.   _____   _____

3. Girls, on the other hand, simply cry and
   appear *helpless*.   _____   _____

4. Studies also show that girls who become
   frightened in a strange room will almost
   invariable move toward their mothers.   _____   _____

5. Boys, though, respond quite *different*.   _____   _____

6. Boys seek something interesting to do
   when they are put in *unfamiliarly* sur-
   roundings.   _____   _____

7. These studies seem to suggest that boys
   are by nature *more autonomous* than girls
   are.   _____   _____

8. But *most* all researchers warn that the results of their studies are at least partly
   based on conditioning.   _____   _____

9. While a boy is still very small, his mother
   makes it *more difficulter* for him to get
   what he wants than she does for a girl.   _____   _____

10. She will quite *typically* throw a toy
    farther away from a boy's reach than from
    a girl's.   _____   _____

31

11. She will be more *protectively* toward a girl than toward a boy.

    _____ _____

12. *Interesting* enough, female monkeys show this same tendency to be more watchful toward their female offspring than they are toward their male offspring.

    _____ _____

13. Many scientists feel quite *certain* that we should observe other primates closely to understand innate differences between men and women.

    _____ _____

14. It is *definitely* a fact that the roles of most male and female ground-dwelling primates are different.

    _____ _____

15. The male usually appears *dominantly* and is charged with the protection of the female and their offspring.

    _____ _____

16. And what may seem *most strangest* of all, the male primate assumes this role even if he is raised apart from adults.

    _____ _____

17. Are male and female differences *genetic* determined then?

    _____ _____

18. Those who argue for genetic determination present their proof *convincingly*.

    _____ _____

19. At the same time, those who feel that male and female differences are determined by the environment argue their case quite *good*.

    _____ _____

20. Throughout history men and women have debated long and *furious* about which sex is superior by nature, and they will probably continue to do so regardless of what studies are conducted.

    _____ _____

5

Use the proper case form to show the function of pronouns or nouns in sentences.

The case of a pronoun is the form it takes to show its function in the sentence as subject of a verb (subjective or nominative case), possessor (possessive case), or object of a verb, verbal, or preposition (objective case). Nouns and some indefinite pronouns (*anyone, someone, everyone*) have a distinctive case form only for the possessive (the *boy's* book, the *boys'* mother: see **15a**), but six of our common pronouns have distinctive forms in all three cases and must be used with care.

SUBJECTIVE	I	we	he, she	they	who
POSSESSIVE	my	our	his, her	their	whose
	(mine)	(ours)	(hers)	(theirs)	
OBJECTIVE	me	us	him, her	them	whom

Note: The personal pronouns *it* and *you* change form only to indicate the possessive—*its, your* (*yours*).

5a Take special care with pronouns in apposition and in compound constructions.

(1) An appositive takes the same case as the noun or pronoun with which it is in apposition.

> We—my sister and *I* (NOT *me*)—share a dormitory room.   [*I* is in the subjective case because it is in apposition with the subject *we*.]
> Let's *you* and *me* (NOT *I*) get an apartment.   ["Let *us*—you and *me*—get an apartment." *Me* and *us* are in the same case.]

Note: Do not let an appositive following a pronoun trick you into making a mistake with case: *We* girls enjoy cooking.

(2) Compound constructions

> My sister and *I* (NOT *me*) often disagree.   [*I* is a subject of the verb.]
> Abner invited both my sister and *me* (NOT *I*).   [*Me* is an object.]

Note: *Myself* (*himself, ourselves*, and so on) is not a substitute for *I* or *me* (*he, us*, and so on); it is a reflexive or intensive pronoun: I hit *myself*; I *myself* will go. Avoid the illiterate forms of reflexive pronouns—*hisself, theirselves*.

5b Determine the case of each pronoun by its use in its own clause.

(1) Pronoun as subject of a clause

The subject of a clause always takes the subjective case, even when the whole clause is the object of a verb or a preposition.

I am impressed by *whoever* is able to write well. [*Whoever* is the subject of *is able. Whoever is able to write well* is the object of *by*.]

I envy *whoever* expresses himself well. [The complete clause *whoever expresses himself well*, not merely the pronoun *whoever*, is the object of *envy*.]

(2) Pronoun followed by a parenthetical *I think, he says*, etc.

Do not allow such parenthetical expressions as *I think, he says, we know* to trick you into changing the subjective *who* (*whoever, whosoever*) to *whom* (*whomever, whomsoever*).

A judge of the Supreme Court must be a man *who* (NOT *whom*) people know is above reproach. [*Who* is the subject of *is.*]

Brandeis was a judge *who* (NOT *whom*) I believe was such a person. [Brandeis was a judge *who* was such a person.]

(3) Pronouns following *than* or *as*

A pronoun following *than* or *as* takes the subjective or objective case according to whether the pronoun is subject or object of an implied verb.

He is older than *I* (*am*).
He likes you as much as (he likes) *me*.
He likes you better than *I* (like you).

5c In formal writing use *whom* for all objects.

For *whom* does he work? [Good usage, formal or informal, always requires the objective *whom* immediately following a preposition.]

Informal English tends to avoid the use of the objective *whom* unless it comes immediately after a preposition: *Who* does he work for?

5d As a rule, use the possessive case immediately before a gerund.

His becoming a doctor pleased his parents.
My parents approved of *my* (*our, his, her, their*) joining the Peace Corps.

5e Use the objective case for the subject, object, or complement of an infinitive.

She invited *me* to visit *her*. [*Me* is the subject and *her* the object of the infinitive *to visit; me to visit her* is the object of the verb *invited*.]

5f Use the subjective case for the complement of the verb *be*.

PATTERN   SUBJECT—LINKING VERB *BE*—COMPLEMENT.

| That | may be | she. |
| It | was | they. |

Note: Informal usage accepts *It is me* (*It's me*).

Case of pronouns

NAME _____ SCORE _____

DIRECTIONS   In the following sentences cross out the incorrect form within parentheses and write the correct form in the blank at the right. After your answers have been checked, read the sentences aloud several times to accustom your ear to the correct pronoun.

EXAMPLE

A man and a woman were debating (who, ~~whom~~) was responsible for the tradition of male superiority.   _who_

1. Both (he and she, him and her) agreed that Judaeo-Christian theology has influenced the development of attitudes toward the sexes.   _____

2. She pointed out to (he, him) that man is depicted by the Bible as the superior sex.   _____

3. "(Whoever, Whomever) studies the Bible is struck by the dominant role man has played," she began.   _____

4. "(We, Us) women have been mistreated," she claimed.   _____

5. "The Bible tells (we, us) women that our original model was Eve," the woman pointed out.   _____

6. "It is clear to (whoever, whomever) considers the story of the creation that man is depicted as superior to woman," she complained.   _____

7. "Adam was created first," she went on; "then Eve was made for (he, him) to enjoy and to protect."   _____

8. "And the Bible suggests that it was woman (who, whom) was responsible for all our sorrows," the woman continued.   _____

9. The woman concluded, "Eve capitulated to Satan and then she led Adam (himself, hisself) to doom also."   _____

10. "But," the man suggested, "you women could use the temptation in the Garden of Eden as an argument for your superiority to (we, us) men."   _____

11. "After all, it was Eve (who, whom) was tempted; Adam apparently surrendered without a fight," the man reminded the woman.   _____

12. (Him, His) arguing for female superiority surprised her.   _____

13. "Well, what can you say to those (who, whom) point out that woman was created second?" she asked. _____

14. "Robert Burns, (who, whom) we know was quite a favorite with the ladies, perhaps gave the best answer," the man replied. _____

15. "His poetry tells you and (I, me) that 'Her [Nature's] prentice han' she tried on man, / An' then she made the lasses, O.'" _____

16. The man pointed out to the woman that there were many men during the age of chivalry (who, whom) we are told held the same opinion that Robert Burns did. _____

17. "It was quite believable to (they, them) that God learned a great deal from his first creation and that he made appropriate changes when he created woman," the man explained. _____

18. "You still have something to explain to other women and (I, me, myself)," the woman broke in. _____

19. "What can you say to make (we, us) feel better about woman's being created from man's rib?" she asked. _____

20. The man replied simply, "It's quite obvious to both you and (I, me) that God could have used Adam's foot." _____

6

Make a verb agree in number with its subject; make a pronoun agree in number with its antecedent.

Singular subjects require singular verbs; plural subjects require plural verbs.[1] Pronouns agree with their antecedents (the words to which they refer) in the same way. Note that in the subject the -*s* ending is the sign of the plural while in the verb it is the sign of the third person singular.

> The true *strength* of a nation *is* hard to define.   [Singular subject—singular verb]
> The true *strengths* of a nation *are* hard to define.   [Plural subject—plural verb]
> The *boy* repairs *his* own car.   [Singular antecedent—singular pronoun]
> The *boys* repair *their* own cars.   [Plural antecedent—plural pronoun]

Single out each subject and its verb and connect them mentally: *strength is, strengths are.* Do the same with each antecedent and its pronoun: *boy ← his, boys ← their.* This practice will make it easy to avoid errors in agreement. If you find it difficult to distinguish verbs and relate them to their subjects, review **1a** and **1b**.

6a   Make a verb agree in number with its subject.

(1) Do not be misled by nouns or pronouns intervening between the subject and the verb or by subjects and verbs with endings difficult to pronounce.

> The *noise* of cars and motor boats *drowns out* (NOT *drown out*) the katydids.
> *Every one* of us *is* (NOT *are*) guilty of noise pollution.
> The *naturalist seeks* (NOT *seek*) a solution.

The number of the subject is not changed by the addition of parenthetical expressions introduced by such words as *with, together with, as well as, no less than, including, accompanied by.*

> *Amos,* together with Joe and David, *was immobilized* with fright.
> *Amos,* like his two brothers, *was* a skydiver.

(2) Subjects joined by *and* are usually plural.

> Our dog and a poodle *were* in the same cage.
> A retriever, a cocker spaniel, and a beagle *were housed* together.

Exceptions: A compound subject referring to a single person or to two or more things considered as a unit is singular.

---

[1] Although verbs do not have number, it is customary to use the terms *singular verb* for verbs with singular subjects and *plural verb* for those with plural subjects.

The quarterback and captain *was injured.* [A single individual was both quarterback and captain.]

Turkey and dressing *is* a popular dish at Thanksgiving. [Two nouns considered as a single entity]

Each or *every* preceding singular subjects joined by *and* calls for a singular verb.

Each counselor and each camper *has been advised* to wear shoes.
Every bramble and thorn *is* a menace to bare feet.

(3) Singular subjects joined by *or, nor, either . . . or, neither . . . nor* usually take a singular verb.

Neither the counselor nor the camper *is* very brave.
Either a frog or a cricket *is* probably *making* the noise.

When the meaning is felt to be plural, informal English occasionally uses the plural verb: "Neither she nor I *were dancing,* for we felt tired."

If one subject is singular and one plural, the verb usually agrees with the nearer subject.

Neither counselor nor campers *were invited.*
Neither campers nor counselor *was invited.*

Either the counselor or I *am* responsible.

Many writers prefer to recast such sentences and thus avoid the problem:

The invitation included neither counselor nor campers.
Either the counselor is responsible or I am. OR One of us is responsible.

(4) When the subject follows the verb (as in sentences beginning with *there is, there are*) special care is needed to determine the subject and to make sure that it agrees with the verb.

On the national scene, there *are* at least six *senators running* for the Presidency.
In our state there *is* only one *candidate* for governor.
There *are* few good *men* available.

Before a compound subject the first member of which is singular, a singular verb is sometimes used.

In one of the new buildings there *is* a *library,* which has no books, and a music *room* and six practice *rooms.*

Note: The expletive *it* is always followed by a singular verb: "It *is* the Indians who really own America." "It *is* the Indian who really owns America."

(5) A relative pronoun used as a subject takes a plural or singular verb to accord with its antecedent.

Boys who *throw* the discus . . . A *boy* who *throws* the discus.

Roy is among the *athletes* who *have competed* in the Olympics. [*Athletes* is the antecedent of *who.*]

Roy is the only *one* of our athletes who *has won* a gold medal.   [*One,* not *athletes,* is the antecedent of *who.* The sentence means, "Of all our athletes Roy is the only *one* who *has won* a gold medal.]

(6) When used as subjects, *each, either, neither, another, anyone, anybody, anything, someone, somebody, something, one, everyone, everybody, everything, nobody, nothing* regularly take singular verbs.

Each *plans* to go to China.
Nobody *wants* to be left behind.
Someone *hopes* to go to Macao.

Everybody *is* excited.
Nobody *cares* to stay long.

None is plural or singular, depending on the other words in the sentence or in the immediately surrounding sentences (the context) which condition its meaning.

None *are* so sure of their knowledge as those who have only a little learning.
None *is* so sure of his knowledge as one who has only a little learning.

Any, all, more, most, and *some* are used with plural and singular verbs in much the same way as *none.*

(7) Collective nouns (and numbers denoting fixed quantity) usually take singular verbs because the group or quantity is usually regarded as a unit.

Our football team *has won* the championship.   [The common use: *team* regarded as a unit]
Our football team *are quarreling* over their different positions.   [Less common: individuals on the team regarded separately]

A thousand bushels *is* a good yield.   [A unit]
A thousand bushels *were crated.*   [Individual bushels]

The number of students *was* small.   [*The number* is regularly taken as a unit.]
A number of students *were* sick.   [*A number* refers to individuals.]

(8) A verb agrees with its subject, not with its predicate noun.

His favorite *meal is* hamburgers and potato chips.
Hamburgers and *potato chips are* his favorite meal.

Such sentences are often better recast so as to avoid the disagreement in number between subject and predicate noun.

His favorite meal consists of hamburgers and potato chips.

(9) Nouns plural in form but singular in meaning usually take singular verbs. In all doubtful cases a good dictionary should be consulted.

Regularly singular   aesthetics, civics, economics, genetics, linguistics, mathematics, measles, mumps, news, physics, semantics
Regularly plural   environs, trousers

Some nouns ending in *-ics* (such as *athletics, acoustics,* and *statistics*) are considered singular when they refer to an organized body of knowledge and plural when they refer to activities, qualities, or individual facts.

Athletics [activity in games] *is required* of every student.
Athletics [various games] *provide* good recreation.

Acoustics *is* an interesting study.
The acoustics of the hall *are* good.

Statistics *is* a science.
The statistics *were* easily *assembled.*

(10) A title of a single work or a word spoken of as a word, even when plural in form, takes a singular verb.

> *The Canterbury Tales is considered* rather plain-spoken even today.
> The London *Times is* a fine newspaper.

6b   Make a pronoun agree in number with its antecedent.

A singular antecedent (one which would take a singular verb) is referred to by a singular pronoun; a plural antecedent (one which would take a plural verb) is referred to by a plural pronoun.

(1) In formal English use a singular pronoun to refer to such antecedents as *man, woman, person, one, anyone, anybody, someone, somebody, everyone, everybody, each, kind, sort, either, neither, no one, nobody.* See also 6a(6).

> A characteristic of modern *woman* is *her* (NOT *their*) desire to be equal in every way to men.

In informal English, plural pronouns are sometimes used after such antecedents when the sense is clearly plural.

> FORMAL   *Each* of the hockey players used *his* own style.
> INFORMAL   *Each* of the hockey players used *their* own style.

(2) Two or more antecedents joined by *and* are referred to by a plural pronoun; two or more singular antecedents joined by *or* or *nor* are referred to by a singular pronoun. If one or two antecedents joined by *or* is singular and one plural, the pronoun usually agrees with the nearer antecedent. See also **6a(2)** and **6a(3).**

> *Sally and Kim* have finished *their* practice teaching.
> Neither *Sally nor Kim* has finished *her* practice teaching.

(3) Collective nouns are referred to by singular or plural pronouns, depending on whether the collective noun is considered singular or plural. See also **6a(7).**

Special care should be taken to avoid making a collective noun *both* singular and plural within the same sentence.

> INCONSISTENT   The fraternity is planning their fall rush program. [*The fraternity* is first considered singular because of the choice of *is* and then plural because of *their.*]
>
> CONSISTENT   The *fraternity is planning its* fall rush program. [Singular]   OR
>   The *fraternity are planning their* fall rush program. [Plural]

Agreement of subject and verb

Exercise 6-1

NAME _____ SCORE _____

DIRECTIONS   In the following sentences underline each subject once and each verb twice. If all verbs in a sentence agree with their subjects, write *C* in the blank at the right; if not, circle the incorrect verb form and enter the correct form of the verb in the blank.

EXAMPLES

There (is) many famous <u>encounters</u> between men and women.   *are*

<u>Each</u> of them <u>tells</u> us something about what <u>we</u> <u>have come</u>   *C*
     to regard as typical male and female behavior.   _____

1. One of the richest sources for famous relationships between men and women is mythology.   _____

2. Among the many famous couples was Zeus and Hera.   _____

3. The king and queen of the gods was almost always depicted as quarreling.   _____

4. The usual cause for their quarrels was another woman.   _____

5. Zeus, like many of the other Greek gods, was typically unfaithful.   _____

6. Whenever one of the beautiful earth women were spotted by Zeus, he would immediately plot her seduction.   _____

7. Hera's reaction to Zeus's escapades are predictable.   _____

8. Her jealousy upon learning of Zeus's latest paramour was the cause of misfortune for many an earth woman.   _____

9. Included in the list of Zeus's seductions was Europa, Leda, and Io.   _____

10. Perhaps the most unfortunate woman of all Zeus's conquests were Io.   _____

11. The news of Zeus's misbehavior, as usual, were eventually relayed to Hera.   _____

12. Neither Zeus nor Hera were ever willing to admit defeat.   _____

13. Zeus's attempt to hide his misconduct from Hera's watchful eyes were the beginning of Io's tragedy.   _____

41

14. Hera's expectations of finding Zeus with a woman was seemingly disappointed when she found Zeus standing beside a cow. _____

15. But the wiles of woman are well known to all who study mythology. _____

16. Hera knew that her suspicion about the true identity of the cow were well founded. _____

17. The thing that Hera chose to request from all of Zeus's possessions was the heifer. _____

18. There was no excuses that Zeus could give for keeping so insignificant a thing as a cow. _____

19. The chances of Zeus's seeing Io again was reduced when Hera set Argus to watch the heifer. _____

20. The number of Argus's eyes, of course, are well known in mythology since the eyes, at Argus's death, became a part of the peacock's tail. _____

21. Zeus's further attempts to see Io in spite of seemingly impossible circumstances testifies to the male's ability to persevere. _____

22. Hermes, one of the cleverest of the gods, were commissioned by Zeus to put the hundred eyes of Argus to sleep. _____

23. A number of stories was told by Hermes in an attempt to put all of Argus's eyes to sleep, and finally one story was successful. _____

24. But Hera discovered Zeus's plan; thus Io's woes was only increased because Hera sent a gadfly to plague her. _____

25. This myth, like many others, suggest that man is typically unfaithful while woman is typically jealous and spiteful. _____

NAME _____ SCORE _____

DIRECTIONS   In each of the sentences below strike out the pronoun in parentheses that fails to agree with its antecedent. Then enter in the blank at the right the antecedent and the correct pronoun.

EXAMPLE

When one reads about the Trojan War, (he realizes, ~~they realize~~) how the relationship between a man and a woman can affect the course of history.   *one — he realizes*

1. Every woman knows that (her, their) sex is credited with many of the misfortunes that have befallen mankind.   _____

2. No one is surprised when (he learns, they learn) that the Trojan War was caused by a woman.   _____

3. Both Paris and Menelaus claimed (his, their) right to Helen, the most beautiful woman in the world.   _____

4. Neither Paris nor Menelaus was willing to relinquish (his, their) claim to Helen.   _____

5. Each had (his, their) reason for claiming Helen: Menelaus was married to her and Paris was promised her by Venus.   _____

6. When Paris carried Helen off to Troy, all of the great Greek warriors pledged (himself, themselves, theirselves) to return her to Menelaus.   _____

7. Helen was apparently one of those women who find (she, they) can adjust to different men.   _____

8. She lived with Paris for ten years while the Greek army spent (its, their) energy trying to break through the walls of Troy.   _____

9. The Greeks won the war with the celebrated Trojan Horse, and each of the surviving warriors returned to (his, their) wife and home.   _____

10. Menelaus was the only one of the warriors who did not have to return to (his, their) wife.   _____

11. Helen accompanied Menelaus back to Sparta, where the couple supposedly lived out (its, their) days in marital bliss.   _____

12. When a person studies this myth, (he, they) may conclude that a man is typically forgiving and a woman typically adaptable.   _____

13. Another famous Greek, Agamemnon, did not find (his, their) return home a pleasant experience.   _____

14. A characteristic of many women in mythology is (her, their) inability to remain faithful.   _____

15. Some Greek women found (herself, themselves, theirselves) lovers during the Trojan War.   _____

16. Clytemnestra, Agamemnon's wife, was among the women who proved (herself, themselves, theirselves) unfaithful.   _____

17. Like many men, Agamemnon was not prepared for the kind of homecoming (he, they) received.   _____

18. Clytemnestra, with the help of her lover, used (her, their) wiles to murder Agamemnon on the very day of his homecoming.   _____

19. A student of mythology often finds (himself, hisself, themselves) reading about a faithless, conniving woman like Clytemnestra.   _____

20. Is a woman, then, basically deceptive in (her, their) dealings, or is mythology simply partial to men?   _____

7

Use the appropriate form of the verb.

The verb is our most inflected part of speech. It changes form to show both tense and number: he *eats*, they *eat*, he or they *ate*. Most verbs have four distinct forms or inflections (*write, writes, writing, written*), but a few have only three (*set, sets, setting*), and some have five or more. The verb *be*, our most irregular verb, has eight inflections: *be, am, is, are, being, was, were, been.*

Many of the errors in verb usage come from failure to distinguish between the present tense, or time, and the past tense. These two forms of the verb, along with the past participle, make up the three "principal parts." If we know the principal parts of a verb—the regular present form (*write*), the simple past (*wrote*), and the past participle (*written*)—we can, with a little thought, use the verb correctly in all six tenses. Note how the six tenses are built on the principal parts of the "irregular" verb *write* and the "regular" verb *use.*

Principal parts

PRESENT	write	use
PAST	wrote	used
PAST PARTICIPLE	written	used

Tenses

PRESENT	I write	I use	
FUTURE	I will write	I will use	[Built on the present]
PAST	I wrote	I used	
PRESENT PERFECT	I have written	I have used	[Built on
PAST PERFECT	I had written	I had used	the past
FUTURE PERFECT	I shall have written	I shall have used	participle]

7a Use the appropriate tense form.

The dictionary lists all verbs under the present form—the first of the three principal parts. For all irregular verbs (such as *write, run, see*) the dictionary gives the past tense (*wrote, ran, saw*), the past participle (*written, run, seen*), and the present participle (*writing, running, seeing*). In the case of regular verbs (such as *use*) the past tense and the past participle, when not given, are understood to be formed in the regular way by adding *d* or *ed*.

> NONSTANDARD   Mike sung in the glee club.   [Past tense desired; dictionary gives *sang* as the correct form for the past tense.]
>
> STANDARD   Mike *sang* in the glee club.

Do not confuse verbs similar in meaning and spelling, such as *lay* and *lie, set* and *sit, raise* and *rise*. The verb *lay* (past, *laid;* past participle, *laid*), meaning to place something, always takes an object.

> The scientist *lays* (OR *is laying*) the moon rocks in the drawer.   [Present]
> Yesterday he *laid* the rocks on the table.   [Past]
> Every day he *has laid* them in a different place.   [Past participle]

The verb *lie* (*lay, lain*), meaning to recline, never takes an object.

> I *lie* (OR *am lying*) in my bunk.   [Present]
> Last week I *lay* in my bunk.   [Past]
> I *have lain* in my bunk daily.   [Past participle]

The verb *set* (*set, set*), meaning to place something, always takes an object.

> Charlie *sets* (OR *is setting*) his muddy boots on the dresser, where he *set* them yesterday, and where he *has* always *set* them.

The verb *sit* (*sat, sat*), meaning to rest on a seat, never takes an object.

> He now *sits* (OR *is sitting*) cross-legged on the floor, where he *sat* yesterday, and where he *has sat* every day.

The verb *raise* (*raised, raised*), meaning to lift something, always takes an object.

> He now *raises* (OR *is raising*) the heaviest barbell. He *raised* it yesterday, and he *has* often *raised* it.

The verb *rise* (*rose, risen*), meaning to get up, never takes an object.

> I *rise* (OR *am rising*) reluctantly this morning. I *rose* reluctantly yesterday, and I often *have risen* reluctantly.

Note: In the passive voice the word that is the object in the active voice becomes the subject: "The moon rocks were laid in the cabinet." Verbs that take no object—such as *lie, sit, rise*—cannot be used in the passive voice.

7b   Use logical tense forms in sequence, focusing on the tense of the main or governing verb.

Make a subordinate verb, an infinitive, or a participle conform logically in time with the main verb.

> He *slept* after he *had finished* (NOT *finished*) cutting the grass.
> He *was sleeping* where the grass *had been* (NOT *was*) cut.
> He hoped *to regain* (NOT *to have regained*) his energy.
> *Having slept* (NOT *sleeping*) for an hour, he *was* still *exhausted*.

Caution: Avoid needless shifts in tense.

> SHIFT   The young artist completed the painting and immediately sells it. [Needless shift from past tense to present tense]
>
> IMPROVED   The young artist *completed* the painting and immediately *sold* it.

NAME _____ SCORE _____

DIRECTIONS   In the following sentences enter the correct form of the verb in the blank within the sentence and also in the numbered space at the right. After your answers have been checked, read the sentences aloud several times to accustom your ear to the correct verb.

Much has been (1) _____ (wrote, written)   1._____
about the adventures of Ulysses after the Trojan War.
Like all the other Greek warriors, he (2) _____   2._____
(set, sat) his course for home after Troy was defeated,
but it was only after he had (3) _____ (rode,   3._____
ridden) out many a storm that he reached his own king-
dom. In fact, it was ten years after he (4) _____   4._____
(began, begun) his trip to Ithaca that he actually arrived
there. Since the war itself had (5) _____ (took,   5._____
taken) ten years, he was gone from home for twenty
years. During all this time Penelope, Ulysses' wife,
(6) _____ (laid, lay) down each night hoping   6._____
that he would return. She was (7) _____   7._____
(gave, given) a great deal of trouble by many suitors, but
she remained faithful to her husband.

Meanwhile Ulysses spent a great deal of time with
two women that he (8) _____ (saw, seen) on   8._____
his return voyage. One of the women was Circe who
(9) _____ (took, taken) pride in her ability to   9._____
subdue men. After she had (10) _____ (gave,   10._____
given) a group of Ulysses' men a great banquet, she
turned them into swine. When another of Ulysses' men
(11) _____ (saw, seen) what had happened, he   11._____
reported his findings to his leader. Ulysses immediately
(12) _____ (laid, lay) plans for rescuing the   12._____

men. With the assistance of Mercury, he was able to (13) _____ (set, sit) at Circe's banquet and yet not be transformed into an animal. Circe's respect for Ulysses (14) _____ (raised, rose) when she found him immune to her many powers. She (15) _____ (become, became) his lover and changed his men back to their normal forms. Then, in a sense, Ulysses did (16) _____ (lay, lie) in Circe's power, for he temporarily lost all interest in returning home.

Eventually, Ulysses returned to his wife, but not before he had (17) _____ (laid, lain) in the arms of still another woman, Calypso. Ulysses might not have (18) _____ (gave, given) his homeland much thought while he was with Calypso had it not been for the prodding of Mercury. Interestingly enough, when Ulysses did return home, he executed all the suitors and all the female servants who had (19) _____ (took, taken) up with the suitors. One wonders what Ulysses would have (20) _____ (did, done) had Penelope been unfaithful to him.

13._____

14._____

15._____

16._____

17._____

18._____

19._____

20._____

NAME _____ SCORE _____

DIRECTIONS In the following sentences strike out every verb form that is incorrectly used and write the correct form in the blank at the right. Enter *C* in the blank after each sentence that contains no verb form incorrectly used.

EXAMPLE

Much has been ~~wrote~~ about Aeneas and Dido.   *written*

1. Aeneas, a Trojan prince who survived the war with the Greeks, was ~~chose~~ by the gods to found Rome.   *Chosen*

2. When Aeneas ~~seen~~ that Troy was lost, he took his father, wife, and son and prepared to flee the city.   *Saw*

3. He was to have experienced many hardships before he reached the country he was to settle.   *C*

4. Even before leaving Troy, he ~~become~~ separated from his wife, and he learned later that she had died during the turmoil of their escape.   *became*

5. Of all the adventures of Aeneas none was more memorable than the time he ~~spends~~ with Dido, the queen of Carthage.   *Spent*

6. Dido was immediately ~~drew~~ to Aeneas because of a spell cast on her by Cupid.   *drawn*

7. When Aeneas recounted the fall of Troy and his wanderings thereafter, Dido began to fall in love with him.   *C*

8. Dido sat quietly listening to Aeneas's stories, and she ~~drunk~~ in every word he spoke.   *drank*

9. Literature is filled with accounts of women like Dido who have ~~fell~~ in love with men because of the adventures they have experienced.   *fallen*

10. Later when Aeneas and Dido were out hunting, a storm arose, and the two ~~seeked~~ shelter in a cave.   *sought*

11. Aeneas was moved by Dido's confession of her love for him, but he ~~knowed~~ that it was not his destiny to remain with her.   *knew*

12. While Aeneas thought about his destiny, the queen of Carthage ~~pledges~~ herself to him forever.   *pledged*

13. As soon as Mercury had ~~spoke~~ to Aeneas about the need to leave Carthage, the Trojan made his plans to depart. _Spoken_

14. He hoped to have departed in secret, but Dido learned of his intentions. _✓_

15. Dido tried desperately to persuade Aeneas to stay, but his mind was set on finding Rome. _c_

16. Even as Ulysses had ~~did~~, Aeneas put his goal before his love for a woman. _done_

17. When Aeneas had ~~went~~, Dido killed herself because she knew that Carthage was destined to become the enemy of the state Aeneas would establish. _gone_

18. As Aeneas sailed away from Carthage, he ~~has seen~~ the funeral pyre of Dido burning on the shore. _Saw_

19. Many writers after Virgil, the author of the *Aeneid,* have ~~ask~~ about the justice of Dido's treatment. _asked_

20. Chaucer, for one, ~~choose~~ to discuss the tragedy of Aeneas's broken vows to Dido. _Chose_

Capitals / Italics   cap 9 / ital 10

9 Capitalize words in accordance with general usage.

First words   Use capitals to mark the beginning of (1) each sentence, even if it is directly quoted within another sentence; (2) each line of poetry; and (3) the title of a book, even if the first word is *a* or *the*.

> My friend asked, "Have you read *The Last of the Mohicans?*"

Proper names   Capitalize words referring to specific persons, places, organizations, races, or things (*Shakespeare, America*); adjectives derived from proper names (*Shakespearean, American*); titles of respect preceding the name of a person (*Captain* Smith, *Senator* Jones); words denoting family relationship when used as titles or alone in place of the name, but not when preceded by a possessive (*Brother* James; a trip with *Father;* a trip with my *father*); and other words used as an essential part of a proper name (Mills *College*, Webster *High School*). But articles, prepositions, and conjunctions used as a part of a proper name are usually not capitalized, except as the first word of the title of a book. The pronoun *I* and the interjection *O* are always capitalized, as are most nouns referring to the Deity (the *Saviour*, the *Almighty*).

Caution: Avoid needless capitals. Note especially that the seasons (*spring, summer, fall, autumn, winter*) are capitalized only when personified, as in poetry; that *north, south, east,* and *west* are capitalized only in referring to a specific region (the history of the *West*); that the names of studies are capitalized only when specific (*history, History 2*) or when derived from a proper name (*Spanish*).

Abbreviations   Abbreviations are usually capitalized or not capitalized according to the capitalization of the word abbreviated: *m.p.h.* (*miles per hour*); *H.R.* (*House of Representatives*); *naut.* (*nautical*); *Pac.* (*Pacific*).

10 Italicize (underline) words in accordance with general usage.

Use italics to indicate titles of books, long plays, or magazines; names of ships and aircraft; foreign words; and letters, figures, or words spoken of as such.

> He read *Treasure Island* while taking a cruise on the *Majestic*.
> He soon became *persona non grata*.
> Drop the *3* from *8763;* then omit *c* to make *fact* read *fat*.

Caution: Use italics sparingly as a means of giving emphasis to a word or a group of words.

11

In ordinary writing avoid most abbreviations, and write out numbers whenever they can be expressed in one or two words.

11a Spell out all titles except *Mr., Messrs., Mrs., Mmes., Dr.,* and *St.* (for *Saint*, NOT for *Street*). These are usually spelled out when not followed by a proper name.

11b Spell out names of states (*Texas*, NOT *Tex.*), countries (*United States*, NOT *U.S.*), months (*August*, NOT *Aug.*), days of the week (*Monday*, NOT *Mon.*), and units of measurement (*pounds*, NOT *lbs.*).

11c Spell out *Street* (*Lee Street*, NOT *Lee St.*), *Road, Park, Company,* and similar words used as part of a proper name.

11d Spell out the words *volume, chapter,* and *page* and the names of courses of study.

> The notes on *chemistry* (NOT *chem.*) are taken from *chapter* 9, *page* 46 (NOT *ch. 9, p. 46,* except in footnotes).

11e Spell out first names (*Charles*, NOT *Chas.*, White).

Permissible Abbreviations: In addition to the abbreviations mentioned in **11a**, the following are permissible and usually desirable: *Jr., Sr., Esq.,* and degrees such as *D.D., LL.D., M.D.,* after proper nouns; A.D., B.C., A.M., P.M., *No.* or *no.,* and *$*, with dates or numerals; *ECA, GOP, RFC, TVA, WAC,* and so on, for names of certain agencies or organizations. The following Latin abbreviations are in general use, but the English terms are often spelled out in formal writing, as indicated in parentheses: *i.e.* (*that is*), *e.g.* (*for example*), *viz.* (*namely*), *cf.* (*compare*), *etc.* (*and so forth*), *vs.* (*versus*). Use *etc.* sparingly. Never write *and etc.; etc.* comes from *et cetera,* of which *et* means *and.*

11f In general spell out numbers that require only one or two words, but use figures for other numbers.

> *twenty* years, *fifty thousand* dollars, *165* years from now, a sum of *$2.27,* *12.5 million* people, exactly *4,568,305* votes

Special Usage Regarding Numbers: Use figures for dates (*1956;* May *1, 1957*); for addresses (*65* Broadway); for identification numbers (Channel *4,* Route *22*); for pages of a book (page *40*); for decimals and percentages (*.57* inches, *10* percent); and for the hour of the day with A.M. or P.M. (*4:00* P.M.). Normally use figures for a series of numbers (a room *25* feet long, *18* feet wide, and *10* feet high). Spell out any numeral at the beginning of a sentence.

Capitals, italics, abbreviations, and numbers

NAME _____ SCORE _____

DIRECTIONS   In the following sentences (1) capitalize where necessary, (2) cross through needless capitals, (3) underline all words that should be italicized, and (4) correct poor usage of abbreviations and numbers. In the blanks at the right enter the correct forms for all words that need to be changed. Write *C* after each line that needs no revision.

EXAMPLE

Aeneas and ~~D~~ido are only one of the famous couples   *Dido*

in mythology.   *C*

1. In ~~C~~ollege courses in ~~L~~iterature and history stu-   _____

   dents read about Henry VIII of england and his 6   _____

   wives.

2. In history 203 at sewanee university students read   _____

   about the lords and ladies of the french court.   _____

3. Perhaps 75% or more of the World's writers have   _____

   talked about the Psychology of male-female rela-   _____

   tionships.

4. The bible, especially chpts. written by Saint Paul,   _____

   has much to say about the duties of men and   _____

   women in the Church and the home.   _____

5. In the 19th. Century the Romantic writers spoke   _____

   often of what today we call "Free Love."   _____

6. In his book sex in human relationships Magnus   _____

   Hirschfeld has written, "love is a conflict between   _____

   reflexes and reflections."

7. During the Spring people in the U.S., as well as   _____

   elsewhere, are usually optimistic enough about   _____

love to sing, "it's love that makes the world go _____
round."

8. The nineteen sixties and nineteen seventies have _____
seen love-ins and signs that read, "make love, not _____
war."

9. Books like *Uncoupling: The Art of Coming Apart* _____
have been #1 sellers at bookstores across the _____
Country. _____

10. The Feb., 1973, issue of McCall's featured "is _____
anyone Faithful any more?"—an article typical of _____
those found in general periodicals as well as _____
Women's Magazines. _____

The Comma ,/ 12

12

Use the comma in order to make clear the meaning of the sentence.

The reading of sentences aloud to determine where pauses and changes in voice pitch naturally come will often show where commas should be placed. But sentence structure is usually a more reliable test.

The many different uses of the comma may be grouped under a very few principles and mastered with comparative ease by anyone who understands the structure of the sentence. These principles, which cover the normal practice of the best contemporary writers, are adequate for the needs of the average college student. He may note that skilled writers sometimes employ the comma in unusual ways to express delicate shades of meaning. Such variations can safely be made only by the writer who has first learned to apply the following major principles:

Use the comma—

a to separate main clauses joined by *and, but, or, nor,* or *for;*
b to set off certain introductory elements;
c to separate items in a series, including coordinate adjectives modifying the same noun;
d to set off parenthetical elements (especially nonrestrictive clauses, phrases, and words).

12a Commas are used between main clauses joined by the coordinating conjunctions *and, but, or, nor, for*.[1]

PATTERN   MAIN CLAUSE, { *and* / *but* / *or* / *nor* / *for* } MAIN CLAUSE.

A picture by Titian sold for almost four million dollars in London, and the man who bought it felt he got a bargain.

The buyer refused to comment on whether the picture would go to America, but art critics believe it inevitably will.

The British National Gallery could not bid high enough, nor was it possible to raise the money from private sources in England.

---

[1] *Yet* is occasionally used as a coordinating conjunction equivalent to *but.* Informal writing frequently uses *so* as a coordinating conjunction, but careful writers usually avoid the *so* sentence by subordinating one of the clauses: see **24b**.

It is hoped that there will be more money available in the future, for it is sad to see Britain lose her long-held art treasures.

Caution: Do not confuse a simple sentence containing a compound predicate (no comma needed) with a compound sentence (comma needed).

Mary iced the birthday cake and served it to her guests. [No pause and therefore no comma needed between the parts of the compound predicate]

Even more objectionable than a comma between parts of a compound predicate is the use of a comma before a conjunction which joins merely two words (*boy* and *girl, pure* and *simple*) or two phrases (*to work* and *to play*) or two subordinate clauses (*that he ran for office* and *that he won*).

At times, the comma is used to set off what seems to be merely the second part of a compound predicate, or even a phrase. Closer examination, however, usually discloses that the material following the comma is actually a main clause with some words "understood"; the use of the comma emphasizes the distinction between the principal ideas in the sentence. Note the following sentences, in which the implied matter is inserted in brackets:

Growing up is largely learning to settle for what is possible, and for the young [growing up] is not always a happy process.   —LONDON TIMES

The clothes of teenagers have changed amazingly in the past ten years, and their ideas [have changed] even more so.

Exceptions to 12a: The comma before the coordinating conjunctions *and* and *or* (and sometimes *but* or *for*) may be omitted if the main clauses are short.

The dog barked and the burglar ran.

A semicolon is often preferable to a comma when the main clauses are very long. The use of the semicolon is strongly desirable, if not absolutely necessary, when one clause contains commas; the semicolon enables the reader to see at a glance the chief break in the sentence. See also **14a**.

The people shall not be deprived or abridged of their right to speak, to write, or to publish their sentiments; and the freedom of the press as one of the great hallmarks of liberty shall be inviolable.   —BILL OF RIGHTS

12b Commas follow such introductory elements as adverb clauses, long phrases, mild interjections, or transitional expressions. (Note that in speaking a pause normally marks such commas.)

PATTERNS   ADVERB CLAUSE, MAIN CLAUSE.
  LONG PHRASE, MAIN CLAUSE.
  INTERJECTION, MAIN CLAUSE.
  TRANSITIONAL EXPRESSION, MAIN CLAUSE.

(1) When an adverb clause precedes the main clause, it is usually followed by a comma.

Although our family had enjoyed the vacation, we were ready to go home. [Read the sentence aloud, and notice the pause after the adverb clause.]

Many writers omit the comma after short introductory clauses, and sometimes after longer ones, when the omission does not make for difficult reading. In the following sentences, the commas may be used or omitted at the option of the writer:

> After it rained (,) the sun shone.
> When he drove (,) he was conscious of the traffic laws. [When the subject of the introductory clause is repeated in the main clause, the comma is usually unnecessary.]

Note: When the adverb clause *follows* the main clause, there is usually no pause and no need for a comma.

> PATTERN   MAIN CLAUSE   ADVERB CLAUSE.
> They were seated before the other couple came.
> We talked until the stars came out.

Such adverb clauses, however, are set off by commas if they are parenthetical or loosely connected with the rest of the sentence—especially if the subordinating conjunction seems equivalent to a coordinating conjunction (or if a distinct pause is required in the reading).

> The new Wimbledon tennis champion won easily, although she was only nineteen. [*Although* is equivalent to *but*.]
> She seemed serene and relaxed, whether she was behind in the match or ahead.

(2) A long phrase preceding a main clause usually requires a comma.

> Inhaling deeply and stretching himself to keep every muscle alert, the champion began the match.   —LONDON TIMES

Introductory phrases containing a gerund, a participle, or an infinitive, even though short, must often be followed by a comma to prevent misreading.

> Because of their decision to strike, the miners walked out.
> After eating, the cat washed her face.

Short introductory prepositional phrases, except when they are transitional expressions, are seldom followed by commas.

> After yesterday's race the horse was lame.
> In case of injury I have insurance.

(3) Use a comma after a transitional expression or a mild interjection at the beginning of a sentence.

> In short, I do not wish to go.
> On the other hand, the trip would be pleasant.

> Oh, I wish he were here.
> Whew, that was close.

12c   Commas are used between items in a series, including coordinate adjectives modifying the same noun.

(1) Items in a series

PATTERNS   ITEM 1, ITEM 2, ITEM 3.

                  ITEM 1, ITEM 2, and ITEM 3.

The water was *clear, blue, quiet.* [Words in a series, form *a, b, c*]

The water was *clear, blue,* and *quiet.* [Form *a, b,* and *c*]

The water was *clear* and *blue* and *quiet.* [Form *a* and *b* and *c*. Commas are omitted when *and* is used throughout the series.]

The men walked *in the rain, in the hail,* and *in the snow.* [Phrases in a series]

That we were tired, that we were hungry, and *that we were lost* was quite evident. [Subordinate clauses in a series]

He arrived, he saw the employer's daughter, and *he took the job.* [Main clauses in a series]

The final comma is often omitted, especially by newspapers, when the series takes the form *a, b,* and *c.* But students are usually advised to use the comma throughout the series, if only because the comma is sometimes needed to prevent confusion.

CONFUSING   Mother baked custard, cherry, raisin and apple pies. [Was the last pie a mixture of raisins and apples?]

CLEAR   Mother baked custard, cherry, raisin, and apple pies. OR

              Mother baked custard, cherry, and raisin and apple pies.

(2) Coordinate adjectives

Adjectives are coordinate and take a comma between them when they modify the same word or word group. Notice in the following examples that the natural pauses between coordinate adjectives are indicated by commas.

a tall, white building [*Tall* and *white* are coordinate adjectives modifying the word *building.*]

a tall, white post office building [*Tall* and *white* modify *post office building,* which is pronounced as a unit.]

Tests for Coordinate Adjectives

Coordinate adjectives ordinarily have a reversible word order; adjectives which are not coordinate do not.

COORDINATE   healthy, happy children [Logical: happy, healthy children]

NOT COORDINATE   six healthy children [Illogical: healthy six children]

Coordinate adjectives may have *and* inserted between them without changing the meaning.

COORDINATE   tall, handsome boys [Logical: tall and handsome boys]

NOT COORDINATE   six tall boys [Illogical: six and tall boys]

12d Commas are used to set off parenthetical elements ("interrupters") such as nonrestrictive words, clauses, and phrases. Restrictive words, clauses, and phrases are not set off.

Use a comma after a parenthetical element at the beginning of a sentence, before a parenthetical element at the end, and both before and after one within a sentence.

My friends, we must guard our liberty.
We must guard our liberty, *my friends.*
We must, *my friends,* guard our liberty.

He repeated, "Liberty is precious."
"Liberty is precious," *he repeated.*
"Liberty," *he repeated,* "is precious."

Caution: When two commas are needed to set off a parenthetical element within the sentence, do not forget the second comma. To use one comma but not the second makes reading more difficult than the omission of both commas does.

CONFUSING   The book, of course will be completed.
CLEAR   The book, of course, will be completed.   OR   The book of course will be completed.

CONFUSING   The book, we have been assured is ready for publication.
CLEAR   The book, we have been assured, is ready for publication.

(1) Nonrestrictive clauses and phrases are set off by commas. Restrictive clauses and phrases are not set off.

Adjective clauses and phrases are nonrestrictive when they merely add information about a word already identified. Such modifiers are parenthetical and may be omitted. Since they are not essential to the meaning of the main clause, they are set off by commas.

William Penn, *who was the leader of the Quakers,* was granted land by Charles II. ["William Penn was granted land by Charles II" is true without the nonessential *who was the leader of the Quakers.*]
Philadelphia, *which Penn founded,* is now a fine city.
Philadelphia, *founded by Penn,* is now a fine city.

Adjective clauses and phrases are restrictive when they are needed to identify the word they modify. Such clauses and phrases limit or restrict the meaning of the sentence and cannot be omitted; therefore no commas should be used.

The man *who led the Quakers* obtained land from Charles II. ["The man obtained land from Charles II" is true only with the essential *who led the Quakers.*]
The city *founded by the Quakers* was Philadelphia.

Adjective clauses beginning with *that* are restrictive. Adjective clauses beginning with *who (whom, whose)* and *which* may be restrictive or nonrestrictive.

Your voice can help you distinguish between restrictive and nonrestrictive modifiers. As you read the following sentences aloud, note that you neither pause nor lower the pitch of your voice for the restrictive passages. On the other hand, you normally "set off" the nonrestrictive modifiers by using definite pauses and by changing the pitch of your voice.

RESTRICTIVE   The person *holding the winning ticket* should come forward.
NONRESTRICTIVE   Helen, *holding the winning ticket,* received the prize.

RESTRICTIVE   A man *who works in a bank* must understand and enjoy figures.
NONRESTRICTIVE   My father, *who works in a bank,* enjoys working with figures.

Carefully study the meaning of the sentences below. Also read each one aloud, and let your voice help you to distinguish between restrictive and nonrestrictive clauses and phrases.

NONRESTRICTIVE

Cairo, *which is on the River Nile,* is a very old city.   [The *which* clause, adding information about a city already identified, is parenthetical and not essential to the main clause, *Cairo is a very old city.* Commas needed.]
Cairo, *situated on the River Nile,* is a very old city.   [Phrase]

RESTRICTIVE

A city *that is old* is often in need of modern improvements.   [The clause *that is old* is essential to the main clause. No commas.]
A city *in need of modern improvements* has hard work ahead.   [Phrase]

NONRESTRICTIVE

My brother, *who is paying his own way through school,* must work every summer.   [The italicized clause adds information about a person already identified. Commas mark pauses and change in voice pitch.]
My brother, *paying his own way through school,* works hard every summer.   [Phrase]

RESTRICTIVE

Any boy *who wants to pay his own way through school* must work hard.   [The *who* clause is essential to the identification of *any boy.*]
Any boy *paying his own way through school* must work hard.   [Phrase]

Sometimes a clause or phrase may be either restrictive or nonrestrictive; the writer signifies his meaning by the proper use of the comma.

NONRESTRICTIVE   He liked his teachers, *who also liked him.*   [He liked all his teachers. In turn, all of them liked him.]
RESTRICTIVE   He liked his teachers *who also liked him.*   [He liked only those teachers who also liked him.]

(2) Nonrestrictive appositives, contrasted elements, geographical names, and items in dates and addresses are set off by commas.

APPOSITIVES AND CONTRASTED ELEMENTS

Appositives are usually nonrestrictive (parenthetical), merely adding information about a person or thing already identified. Such appositives are set off by commas, which mark distinct pauses and changes in voice pitch. Note that most appositives may be readily expanded into nonrestrictive clauses. In other words, the principle underlying the use of commas to set off nonrestrictive clauses also applies here.

Lynn, *my nephew*, is now in India.   [The appositive *my nephew* is equivalent to the nonrestrictive clause *who is my nephew*. Note the distinct pauses and changes in voice pitch.]

Ulysses S. Grant, *the victorious general in the Civil War*, was later a mediocre president.   [The appositive is equivalent to the nonrestrictive clause *who was the victorious general in the Civil War*.]

My companions were James White, *Esq.*, William Smith, *M.D.*, and Rufus L. Block, *Ph.D.*   [Abbreviated titles after names are treated as appositives.]

Our dreams, *not our failures*, should direct our future lives.   [The contrasted element is a sort of negative appositive.]

My cousin, *not my nephew*, has the key.

High grades come from hard work, *not from idleness*.

At times appositives are restrictive, and commas are omitted.

My nephew *Lynn* is the one who is in India.   [*Lynn*, not some other nephew, is in India.]

The victor *Grant* was not as outstanding as a president as he had been as a general.   [*Grant* restricts the meaning, telling what victor was not as outstanding a president as he had been a general.]

George *the Third* was King of England in 1771.   [An appositive that is part of a title is restrictive.]

The word *decibels* has come into increasing use in recent years.

Both Francis Bacon *the philosopher* and Francis Bacon *the painter* have contributed to man's understanding of his world.

GEOGRAPHICAL NAMES, ITEMS IN DATES AND ADDRESSES

Knoxville, Tennessee, lies at the foot of the Smoky Mountains.   [*Tennessee* may be thought of as equivalent to the nonrestrictive clause *which is in Tennessee*.]

Send the letter to Mr. J. L. Karnes, Clayton, Delaware 19938.   [The zip code is not separated by a comma from the name of the state.]

Wednesday, July 20, 1971, in Rome   [Students are usually advised not to drop the comma after the year, as in "July 20, 1971 in Rome."]

October, 1822, in Boston   OR   October 1822 in Boston   [Commas are often omitted when the day of the month is not given.]

(3) Parenthetical words, phrases, or clauses (inserted expressions), words in direct address, and absolute elements are set off by commas.

PARENTHETICAL EXPRESSIONS

Actually, the term "parenthetical" is correctly applied to all nonrestrictive elements discussed under **12d**; but the term is more commonly applied to such expressions as *on the other hand, in the first place, in fact, to tell the truth, however, that is, for example, I hope, I report, he says*. The term would apply equally well to expressions inserted in dialogue: *he said, he observed, he* *protested,* and so on. Parenthetical expressions that come at the beginning of a sentence are treated in both **12b** and **12d**.

> Students without funds, *for example,* may now borrow money easily.
> The judge held, *in fact,* that the firm was liable.
> We must, *on the other hand,* consider our budget.
> "The next meeting," *she announced,* "will be today."
> The rest of the activities, *however,* were canceled. [When *however* means "nevertheless," it is usually set off by commas.]
> Use seat belts *however* well you drive. [When *however* means "no matter how," it is not parenthetical and therefore is not set off by commas.]

Parenthetical expressions causing little if any pause in reading are frequently not set off by commas: *also, too, indeed, perhaps, at least, likewise,* and so forth. The writer must use his own judgment.

> Sewing is *indeed* a useful hobby.
> The boat *perhaps* will be repaired by Saturday.
> Government aid is *of course* needed. OR Government aid is, *of course,* needed.

DIRECT ADDRESS

> Here, *Susan,* is your mistake.
> This, *fellow members,* will be our club project.
> I appeal, *sir,* to your sense of fair play.

ABSOLUTE ELEMENTS

Expressions independent of the rest of the sentence are called absolute elements.

> *Rain or shine,* the mail must go through. [Absolute phrase]
> He had no intention of stopping, *his mind being made up.* [Nominative absolute]
> *Well,* we will hope for the best. [Mild interjection]
> There is no mail, *is there?* [Echo question]

12e Occasionally a comma, though not called for by any of the major principles already discussed, may be needed to prevent misreading.

Use **12e** sparingly to justify your commas. In a general sense, nearly all commas are used to prevent misreading or to make reading easier. But your mastery of the comma will come largely through application of the more specific major principles (*a, b, c, d*) to the structure of the sentence.

> CONFUSING Outside the trees were weighted with snow. [*Outside* may be at first mistaken for a preposition.]
> CLEAR Outside, the trees were weighted with snow. [*Outside* is clearly an adverb.]
> CONFUSING Above all the guests must be made to feel welcome.
> CLEAR Above all, the guests must be made to feel welcome.

Commas between main clauses   Exercise 12-1

NAME _____ SCORE _____

DIRECTIONS In the following sentences, insert an inverted caret (V) between main clauses and add a comma or semicolon as needed; in the blank at the right enter the comma or the semicolon plus the coordinating conjunction. If the sentence is correct, write C in the blank at the right. (Note that some of the sentences are not compound. Bracket any subordinate clauses that appear incidentally.)

EXAMPLE

Mark Antony, like Aeneas, had a goal, ᵛbut unlike Aeneas, he was willing to sacrifice everything [when he fell in love.]   *,(or;) but*

1. Antony was a brave warrior and a strong leader but he met his match in Cleopatra.   _____

2. In youth Cleopatra was the lover of Caesar and in middle age she became the lover of Antony.   _____

3. Many descriptions of Cleopatra's charm have been presented but none is more famous than the one penned by Shakespeare.   _____

4. When Enobarbus, a servant of Antony, saw Cleopatra on her lavish barge, he knew that Antony would become her servant and would never leave her.   _____

5. Enobarbus said of Cleopatra, "Age cannot wither her" nor, he continued, can "custom stale / Her infinite variety."   _____

6. Enobarbus recognized that "other women cloy the appetites they feed" but Cleopatra, he claimed, "makes hungry / Where most she satisfies."   _____

7. Enobarbus' prediction of Antony's enslavement to Cleopatra's charm came true for Antony twice deserted battles to follow his love.   _____

8. Antony's military forces, who were willing to follow their leader anywhere, were experienced only in land battles but Cleopatra, using her feminine guile, was able to persuade Antony to fight at sea.   _____

9. Antony could not resist Cleopatra's charm nor could he remain to fight when Cleopatra deserted the battle, even though their forces were winning. _____

10. After Antony lost the second battle against Octavious Caesar's forces, he became convinced that Cleopatra was in league with Octavius and that she had deserted the battle knowing that Antony would follow her. _____

11. Antony decided that the Queen of Egypt should die but Cleopatra was quick to plot a course of reconciliation. _____

12. She sent word to Antony that she had killed herself for love of him and that her body lay inside the great monument she had built for herself. _____

13. Antony believed the message and ran upon his own sword but he did not succeed in killing himself instantly. _____

14. He died later in Cleopatra's arms and then the Queen of Egypt quickly planned her own death. _____

15. Since Cleopatra could not live without Antony, she used the bite of a poisonous asp to end her life and thus she insured, at least in her own mind, her reunion with her lover. _____

16. Antony and Cleopatra were strong individuals who quarreled often but who were so mutually attracted that they could not live without each other. _____

Commas after introductory clauses or phrases   Exercise 12-2

NAME _____ SCORE _____

DIRECTIONS   Bracket introductory subordinate clauses and underline introductory phrases. After each introductory clause or phrase write a comma or a zero (0), according to whether you think the comma is desirable or not. Also write the comma or the zero in the blank at the right.

EXAMPLES

When analyzing the famous love relationships in literature, one
cannot overlook Romeo and Juliet.   ,

Of all the famous lovers Romeo and Juliet are probably the best
known.   0

1. In the 1970's a movie was made of Shakespeare's *Romeo and Juliet*.   _____

2. Defying traditional theatrical procedure the director of the movie cast a young girl and boy in the lead roles.   _____

3. In Shakespeare's play Romeo and Juliet are indeed young, Juliet being no more than fourteen.   _____

4. When Romeo attends a masked banquet at the home of Juliet's parents he risks his life; for Romeo's parents, the Montagues, and Juliet's, the Capulets, are enemies.   _____

5. At first sight of each other Romeo and Juliet fall in love.   _____

6. After dancing with Juliet Romeo declares, "I ne'er saw true beauty till this night."   _____

7. Later in the evening he manages to steal a kiss from Juliet.   _____

8. Unaware of Romeo's true identity Juliet professes her love for Romeo to her nurse.   _____

9. Upon learning that the young man she has fallen in love with is an enemy of her family Juliet exclaims, "My only love, sprung from my only hate! / Too early seen unknown, and known too late!"   _____

10. When the young couple meet later in the Capulets' orchard Juliet tells Romeo, "O, be some other name! / What's in a name? That which we call a rose / By any other name would smell as sweet."   _____

11. In spite of their families' quarrel the couple pledge eternal love to each other. _____

12. Regardless of the circumstances the couple are determined to marry. _____

13. Immediately after their secret marriage tragedy ensues, for Romeo is forced into killing Juliet's cousin, Tybalt. _____

14. Although she is greatly grieved by the death of Tybalt Juliet still longs to see her young husband. _____

15. Enjoying but one night of love the couple are then parted, for Romeo must go into exile. _____

16. To avoid the marriage her family has planned for her Juliet takes a potion which simulates death. _____

17. Because Romeo thinks that Juliet is truly dead he decides to die himself by her side. _____

18. Drinking poison he lies down beside her. _____

19. As soon as Juliet recovers from the sleeping potion and finds her young husband dead she stabs herself with a dagger. _____

20. Unlike Antony and Cleopatra Romeo and Juliet never quarreled, but perhaps that was because they were young and their love was short-lived. _____

Commas between items in series and coordinate adjectives

NAME _____ SCORE _____

DIRECTIONS   Identify each series by writing *1, 2, 3* above the items and in the blanks at the right. Insert commas where they belong in the sentences and in the blanks at the right. Write *C* after each sentence that needs no revision.

EXAMPLES

Jealous women in literature, history, and mythology are quite common.   <u>1, 2, 3</u>

But the best known of jealous, suspicious characters is a man.   <u>1, 2</u>

1. Othello differs from the woman he marries in age nationality and race.   _____

2. Othello is a courageous fighter and an able strategist who leads the Venetian forces against the Turks.   _____

3. Because of the stirring accounts of his battles and travels that Othello tells, Desdemona, a young beautiful Venetian girl, falls in love with him.   _____

4. Desdemona elopes with Othello in spite of the prolonged angry protest of her father.   _____

5. In the beginning Othello is shown to be a patient loving husband.   _____

6. Unfortunately he has in his service a man who despises him but whom he refers to as honest loyal Iago.   _____

7. Othello unknowingly wounded Iago's pride when he appointed another younger man to the post Iago hoped to have.   _____

8. Iago knows that Othello is basically a good man that he easily misjudges people and that he is insecure about his merits as a husband.   _____

9. Iago decides to use these three quite ordinary traits of Othello to obtain vengeance for the obvious terrible injustice he feels Othello has done him.   _____

10. Iago is a brilliant cunning master of treachery who can manipulate people to do his bidding.   _____

11. Iago's slow painstaking plan to make Othello suspect Desdemona of infidelity takes shape. _____

12. Othello is not quick to doubt Desdemona's faithfulness, but he cannot maintain a calm clear mind in the face of Iago's subtle accusations. _____

13. Iago is always present planting doubt offering suggestions and showing what seems to be proof of Desdemona's infidelity. _____

14. Eventually Othello believes Iago and agrees to smother the innocent sleeping Desdemona. _____

15. Desdemona awakens sees her husband and pleads for her life and a chance to prove her innocence. _____

16. But Othello is now too angry too set on Desdemona's death to listen. _____

17. Desdemona remains an unbelievably kind innocent woman, for her last words to her nurse are that Othello is innocent of her death. _____

18. Othello soon learns of Iago's treachery of his wife's faithfulness and of his own insane jealousy. _____

19. Knowing that he has become a victim of the "green-ey'd monster" and that he has committed a vile unforgivable sin, Othello stabs himself. _____

20. In contrast with the myths we examined, the male characters in literature have so far been depicted as jealous overly romantic and even subservient. _____

Commas to set off parenthetical and nonrestrictive elements

NAME _____ SCORE _____

DIRECTIONS   Insert the commas needed to set off all parenthetical and nonrestrictive elements. In the space at the right enter (1) a dash followed by a comman (–,) to show a nonrestrictive or parenthetical element at the beginning of the sentence, (2) a dash enclosed within commas (,–,) to show a nonrestrictive or parenthetical element within the sentence, and (3) a dash preceded by a comma (,–) to show a nonrestrictive or parenthetical element at the end of the sentence.

EXAMPLES

One of the greatest lovers in English literature is Don Juan, the hero of a comic epic by Lord Byron.   , –

Juan, who comes from a wealthy Spanish family, is destined to love many women but to lose them all.   , – ,

Having reached the age of sixteen, Juan falls madly in love for the first time.   – ,

1. Juan falls in love with Donna Julia a young woman he has known since he was a child.   _____

2. Julia who is married to Don Alfonso is seven years older than Juan.   _____

3. Married to a man who is fifty Julia is naturally attracted to the young, handsome Juan.   _____

4. Not realizing the cause of his pensiveness Juan wanders aimlessly about the woods near his home.   _____

5. He is given to long periods of melancholy during which he ponders the timeless questions of the universe.   _____

6. Sometimes Juan unaware of the passage of time quite forgets to eat.   _____

7. As anyone who has lived for many years knows Juan exhibits all the symptoms of being hopelessly in love.   _____

8. Then on a summer's day an appropriate season for love Juan and Julia find themselves alone together.   _____

9. Julia though she feels herself perfectly innocent flirts openly with Juan.   _____

10. Byron suggests that of course it is woman who initiates romance.   _____

11. Following his companion's lead Juan tries to make love to Julia. _____

12. Julia resists only a little murmuring, "I will ne'er consent"; nevertheless, she consents. _____

13. About midnight Don Alfonso suspecting his wife's infidelity arrives with a lawyer and several witnesses. _____

14. They search almost everywhere without success not thinking to look "*in* the bed as well as under." _____

15. Always prepared for any situation Julia screams accusations at Alfonso. _____

16. Julia like any other woman according to Byron knows how to attack when she is under attack. _____

17. Alfonso is ready to give up the search in despair totally subdued by Julia's tongue. _____

18. At this point however a man's shoe is found, and Juan is soon discovered. _____

19. Juan departs from Cadiz Spain to see other parts of the world. _____

20. Julia is sent to a convent from which she sends Juan a sentimental letter about the difference between men and women when they fall in love. _____

NAME _____ SCORE _____

DIRECTIONS   Insert all necessary commas, justifying each comma by writing above it (and in the space at the right) *a* (main clauses), *b* (introductory element), *c* (series or coordinate adjectives), or *d* (parenthetical element or nonrestrictive clause or phrase), in accordance with the principles explained in Section **12**.

EXAMPLE

Byron believed, as Julia's letter reveals, that men and women have different, conflicting views of love.   *d d c*

1. Men Julia notes have many goals to pursue such as fame power and money; but women have only one goal.   _____

2. Women seek according to Julia only love and they stake their whole existence on it.   _____

3. When a woman loses the one she loves there is nothing more for her to live for except another love relationship.   _____

4. She may love again but the result as Julia sees it is always the same.   _____

5. On board the ship that will take him away from Spain Juan takes out Julia's letter and reads it again.   _____

6. While Juan stands on the deck the wind blowing in his face he opens his heart to the waves and cries openly for his loss of Julia.   _____

7. The more he thinks about Julia and her letter the more seasick he becomes and eventually he can lament his loss no longer because of his upset stomach.   _____

8. Later when a strong ever-changing wind wrecks the ship the crew and passengers board a lifeboat hoping to paddle to shore.   _____

9. Only Juan is destined to see land for the other occupants of the boat starved and thirsty turn cannibals and devour not only Juan's dog but also his tutor.   _____

10. To be sure they are punished for their cannibalism when losing control of their senses they drink sea water ravenously and die howling grinning and swearing.   _____

11. Juan is eventually washed ashore on an island in the Aegean where he meets Haidée the daughter of the pirate who controls the island. _____

12. Juan and Haidée's relationship set among the beauty and isolation of nature is idyllic for it meets all Byron's qualifications for true love. _____

13. Haidée has no qualms about love nor does she who has never known falsehood expect any promises of constancy or marriage from Juan. _____

14. Haidée unlike Julia is "nature's bride" and she loves passionately and openly unconcerned about society's standards. _____

15. While Byron is describing the beautiful innocent relationship of Juan and Haidée he takes time for a few additional comments about other more typical relationships. _____

16. Man Byron says is always unfair to woman who consequently has nothing to look forward to except "a thankless husband" and then "a faithless lover." _____

17. Everything is perfect for Juan and Haidée—that is until Lambro Haidée's father returns to the island. _____

18. Finding Juan and Haidée in each other's arms Lambro wounds Juan and then has the young man bound and carried away. _____

19. Haidée who has tried to intervene falls into a coma from which she never recovers thus spared from becoming like other women who have lost their lovers. _____

20. Juan although severely wounded recovers to travel far away to other lands and other loves. _____

13

Do not use superfluous commas.

Necessary commas indicate appropriate pauses and changes in voice pitch and thus help to clarify the meaning of a sentence. Unnecessary or misplaced commas, however, are false or awkward signals and often confuse the reader. Read the following sentences aloud to note how distinct pauses and changes in voice pitch indicate the need for commas.

> Boys, go to the gymnasium at two o'clock.   [Comma needed to indicate the distinct pause in direct address: see **12d**.]
> The boys go to the gymnasium at two o'clock.   [No commas needed]
>
> Helen enjoys tennis but ⊙ she cannot play well.   [Misplaced comma]
> Helen enjoys tennis, but she cannot play well.   [Comma needed before the coordinating conjunction, where the pause comes: see **12a**.]

If you have a tendency to use unnecessary commas, consider every comma you are tempted to use and omit it unless you can justify it by one of the principles treated under Section **12**. You may be helped also by the following suggestions.

13a   Do not use a comma to separate the subject from its verb or the verb from its object.

In the following sentences the encircled commas should be omitted.

> Americans abroad ⊙ are often very poor ambassadors for their own country. [Needless separation of subject and verb]
> He knew when he was only a boy ⊙ that politeness is important.   [Needless separation of verb and object]
> Some people believe ⊙ that "God Bless America" should be our national anthem.   [Indirect discourse: needless separation of verb and object]

Note: A comma before the verb sometimes makes for clarity when the subject is heavily modified.

> Americans who go to other countries expecting the same knowledge of the English language and the same air conditioning, ice water, and private baths found in hotels in the United States, are often very poor ambassadors for their own country.

13b   Do not use a comma to separate two words or two phrases joined by a coordinating conjunction.

In the following sentences the encircled comma should be omitted.

> The rise in crime is attributed to drugs ⊙ and organized crime.

I leaned over the parapet ⊚ and looked at the city spread out below me. [Compound predicate: *and* joins two verbs.]

He hoped to buy a new car ⊚ and to sell his old one. [*And* joins two infinitive phrases.]

13c   Do not use commas to set off words or short phrases (especially introductory ones) that are not parenthetical or that are very slightly so.

In the following sentences the encircled commas should be omitted.

Next week ⊚ I will go to a wedding ⊚ also.

Maybe ⊚ I should attend the meeting ⊚ too.

In the future ⊚ I expect to stay in school.

13d   Do not use commas to set off restrictive (necessary) clauses, restrictive phrases, or restrictive appositives.

In the following sentences the encircled commas should be omitted.

People ⊚ in glass houses ⊚ should not throw stones.   [Restrictive phrase: no commas needed]

A man ⊚ who lives in a glass house ⊚ should not throw stones.   [Restrictive clause]

My friend ⊚ Bill ⊚ threw a stone.   [Restrictive appositive]

13e   Do not use a comma before the first or after the last item of a series.

Andrea did a study of famous women such as ⊚ Cleopatra, Dido, and Josephine.   [Needless comma before first item of a series]

The sensuous, strong-willed ⊚ Cleopatra attracted both Julius Caesar and Mark Antony.   [Needless comma after last adjective in a series]

NAME _____ SCORE _____

DIRECTIONS   Bracket all subordinate clauses in the following correctly punctuated sentences. In the first blank indicate the type of subordinate clause: adjective (*adj*), adverb (*adv*), or noun (*n*). In the second blank indicate by rule number and letter (see Sections **12** and **13**) why a comma is or is not used with the clause.

	Clause	*Rule*
EXAMPLE		
There are many women in literature [who are as fickle as Don Juan.]	*adj*	13 d

1. "La Belle Dame Sans Merci," which means "The Beautiful Lady Without Pity," is a narrative poem about a fickle woman.   _____ _____

2. Any man who sees "La Belle Dame" is destined to fall in love with her.   _____ _____

3. The lover does not realize that "La Belle Dame" can never remain true to anyone.   _____ _____

4. As soon as the man becomes her slave, she disappears.   _____ _____

5. The man is always lonely and heartsick when he discovers his loss.   _____ _____

6. In John Keats's poem the lover seems near death because he has lost his beautiful lady.   _____ _____

7. He has been enslaved by the same beautiful woman who conquered great kings and warriors in the past.   _____ _____

8. That "La Belle Dame" is a symbol for death or devotion to an ideal is certainly likely.   _____ _____

9. But she may also be viewed as a representation of fickleness, a trait which all too often is associated with women.   _____ _____

10. John Donne wrote a poem about searching for a woman who could remain faithful to one man.   _____ _____

11. Beauty is a quality that can often be found in women, Donne claimed.   _____ _____

12. But, according to Donne, whoever seeks to find a faithful woman may as well try to catch a falling star.   _____ _____

13. If a man should find this rarity, a faithful woman, and report his finding, Donne would not go to see her.   _____ _____

14. Before he could arrive to see the phenomenon, the woman would already have taken a lover or two.   _____ _____

15. Of course, Donne wrote during a period when unfaithfulness was supposedly in vogue.   _____ _____

16. Many of the poets of the seventeenth century recommended that lovers certainly not remain faithful to each other.   _____ _____

17. The familiar line by Robert Herrick, "Gather ye rosebuds while ye may," presented the typical poet's advice of the day to young women.   _____ _____

18. Andrew Marvell, whose best-known poem is "To His Coy Mistress," argued convincingly against chastity.   _____ _____

19. "To His Coy Mistress" presents all the time-honored reasons why a young woman should submit to her lover.   _____ _____

20. Since sex has always been one of the public's favorite subjects, one should not be surprised to discover many unfaithful women and men in literature.   _____ _____

NAME _____ SCORE _____

DIRECTIONS   Explain each comma used properly by writing above it (and in the space at the right) *a* (main clauses), *b* (introductory element), *c* (series or coordinate adjectives), or *d* (parenthetical element or nonrestrictive clause or phrase), in accordance with the principles explained in Section 12. If you cannot justify the use of the comma by one of these principles, indicate that the comma is superfluous by circling it and by entering an encircled comma in the space at the right.

EXAMPLE

Robert Browning, a nineteenth-century poet, wrote about couples like the Duke and Duchess of Ferrara and Andrea del Sarto and his wife.   *d d* ⊙ ⊙

1. Although Browning was happily married himself, many of his poems deal with unhappy marriages, and their causes. _____   _____

2. One unhappily married man, whom Browning wrote about, was the Duke of Ferrara, a figure perhaps drawn from history. _____   _____

3. The Duke, a vain, cruel man, reveals the history of his relationship to his dead wife, to an emissary from his future bride. _____   _____

4. He tells the emissary, who has been invited to view a painting of the Duchess, that his late wife was too friendly, and too quick to praise. _____   _____

5. In fact, she was known to be grateful for the sunset, for a ride on a mule, even for a bough of cherries; but, according to the Duke, she should have been grateful, only, for his gifts to her. _____   _____   _____

6. The Duke is especially proud of his nine-hundred-year-old name, and he obviously feels, that the Duchess was not impressed enough by it. _____

7. Because she smiled at everyone she met, the Duke accused her of being a flirt, and he decided to end her smiles altogether. _____   _____

8. Obviously a victim of extreme jealousy, the Duke had the Duchess either locked up, or killed. _____   _____

9. The Duchess was probably a kind, affectionate, happy, person; but the Duke, annoyed by her good traits, was, and still is, interested only in what can be owned. _____

10. The picture, that he had painted of the Duchess, obviously means more to him than the live Duchess did because he owns the painting. _____

11. In another poem, Browning describes the marital unhappiness of a painter, Andrea del Sarto, and his wife. _____

12. The painter is so devoted to his wife, that he will do anything to please her, even steal for her. _____

13. While he pours out his soul to her, she waits impatiently for her lover, whom the painter is supporting. _____

14. Although the painter realizes that his failures as an artist, are a result of his own lack of vision, he does believe that he could have done better work, if he had had the support of his wife. _____

15. The painter, like many other men, has risked his very soul for love, but his wife feels disgust, not love, in return. _____

16. Browning's male character in "Porphyria's Lover," settles his love problem in a frightening, bizarre way. _____

17. When Porphyria comes to visit him one night, he decides that he will insure her future fidelity, by killing her. _____

18. He winds her hair around her throat, and strangles her, after which he props her head against his shoulder. _____

19. Sitting with her head against his shoulder all night, he convinces himself that he has done the right thing; for God, he boasts, "has not said a word." _____

20. Porphyria's lover is, of course, insane, but then it has been said, that love itself is a kind of madness. _____

14

Use the semicolon (a) between two main clauses not joined by a coordinating conjunction (*and, but, or, nor, for*) and (b) between coordinate elements containing commas. (Use the semicolon only between parts of equal rank.)

In speaking, the pause required for the semicolon is almost as full as that for a period; in fact, the semicolon is sometimes called a weak period. The pause test can help you place the semicolon as well as the comma, but you should rely chiefly on your knowledge of the structure of the sentence.

14a   Use the semicolon between two main clauses not joined by a coordinating conjunction or between two main clauses joined by a coordinating conjunction but containing a great deal of internal punctuation.

PATTERN   MAIN CLAUSE; MAIN CLAUSE

It is not the good that one takes such care to conceal; it is the vicious and unworthy that most people sweep under the rug.

We have enjoyed learning to maneuver a canoe, a sailfish, and a sunfish; but we have had more fun with our catamaran than with any other type of boat.

Note: Use a semicolon between two main clauses joined by a conjunctive adverb or a transitional phrase.

PATTERN   MAIN CLAUSE; $\left\{ \begin{array}{c} conjunctive\ adverb \\ or \\ transitional\ phrase \end{array} \right\}$ MAIN CLAUSE

There was a fascination for him in studying hard; nevertheless, he was aware of a vague unhappiness.

Passing the bar examination took all his thoughts; as a result, finding the girl faded into the background.

14b   Use the semicolon to separate a series of equal elements which themselves contain commas.

At camp Susan signed up for swimming, which everybody had to take; crafts, which she enjoyed the most; and riding, which she really needed to improve.

14c   Use the semicolon between parts of equal rank only, not between a clause and a phrase or a main clause and a subordinate clause.

PARTS OF EQUAL RANK   The rattler was coiled to strike; the biology class approached it with caution.   [Two main clauses]

PARTS OF UNEQUAL RANK   Because the rattler was coiled to strike, the biology class approached it with caution.   [Subordinate clause and main clause separated by a comma]

15

Use the apostrophe (a) to indicate the possessive case—except for personal pronouns, (b) to mark omissions in contracted words or numerals, and (c) to form certain plurals.

15a   Possessives—except for personal pronouns

(1) For words (singular or plural) not ending in an *s* or *z* sound, add the apostrophe and *s* ('s).

> The man's hat, the boy's shoes   [Singular]
> Men's hats, women's dresses   [Plural]
> One's hat, anybody's coat   [Indefinite pronouns—singular]

(2) For plural words ending in an *s* or *z* sound, add only the apostrophe.

> Ladies' hats (hats for ladies), boys' shoes (shoes for boys)

(3) For singular words ending in an *s* or *z* sound, add the apostrophe and *s* ('s) for words of one syllable. For words of more than one syllable, add only the apostrophe unless the second *s* is to be pronounced.

> James's book, Moses' commands, Sartoris's dream

(4) Compounds or nouns in joint possession show the possessive in the last word only.

> My father-in-law's house, someone else's hat, Helen and Mary's room

15b   Do not use the apostrophe with the personal pronouns (*his, hers, its, ours, yours, theirs*) or with the relative-interrogative pronoun *whose*. Note especially that *it's* means *it is*.

> *It's* cold today.   [*It is* cold today.]
> Virtue is *its* own reward.

15c   Omissions in contractions

> Can't, didn't, he's (he is), it's (it is), you're (you are), o'clock (of the clock), the class of '55 (1955).

Notice that the apostrophe is placed exactly where the omission occurs.

15d   Plurals of letters, figures, symbols, and words referred to as words

> Congreve seldom crossed his *t*'s, his 7's looked like 9's, and his *and*'s were usually &'s.

Semicolons

NAME _____ SCORE _____

DIRECTIONS In the following sentences insert an inverted caret (∨) between main clauses and add semicolons as needed. In the blank at the right copy the semicolon and the word or expression immediately following. Write *C* if the sentence is correct. (Bracket any subordinate clause that appears incidentally.)

EXAMPLES

In real life women and men frequently disagree,∨ and their conflict is reflected in literature.   *C*

In "The Forsaken Merman," [which was written by Matthew Arnold,] the man and woman have different priorities in life∨;consequently, their love is a tragic one.   ; consequently

1. Margaret, in "The Forsaken Merman," is the wife of a merman, but she herself is human.   _____

2. She and her husband have several children yet she leaves both her husband and her children.   _____

3. At Easter Margaret hears the toll of a church bell, and since she fears the loss of her soul, she leaves her family to go to the church to pray.   _____

4. Margaret promises she will return soon, however, she becomes too caught up in the human world to leave it.   _____

5. Standing outside the window of Margaret's home, her children cry out to her, begging her to return with them to the sea, but Margaret, who feels she belongs in the world of churches and houses, will not go with them.   _____

6. She loves her children dearly, nevertheless, she has set duty above love.   _____

7. The merman knows he has lost his wife forever, thus he calls the children to come away with him.   _____

8. In reading the poem by Matthew Arnold, one tends to side with the merman, who feels that love is more important than duty.   _____

9. Matthew Arnold wrote many poems about love, in fact, he often presented love as the only hope for men and women.   _____

10. In "The Buried Life," for example, Arnold extols the value of a love relationship. _____

11. One can understand himself only through loving another, that is, he can see his personality reflected in the eyes of his true love. _____

12. In many other poems, too, one sees Matthew Arnold's high regard for love, in such a poem as "Dover Beach," for example. _____

13. The speaker in "Dover Beach" looks across the channel to the lights on the French coast, and he describes what seems to be a lovely, tranquil setting. _____

14. The sea only seems to be calm it is, in fact, turbulent, as one realizes when he listens to the sound of the surf. _____

15. Life is as deceptive as the sea, the speaker reasons, it presents the same façade of beauty and tranquility. _____

16. The world is, in reality, a desperate place, where there is no joy, no faith, and no peace. _____

17. The speaker describes the world in very unpleasant terms, for instance, he likens it to a battlefield at night. _____

18. A man should not turn to the world for hope, instead he should look to his love. _____

19. The speaker feels that the world offers him nothing but pain, thus he cries out to his love, "Let us be true / To one another." _____

20. The love the speaker has for his love cannot change the world, however, it can give some meaning to life. _____

Apostrophes   Exercise 15-1

NAME _____ SCORE _____

DIRECTIONS   In the sentences below insert all necessary apostrophes. In the blanks at the right enter each word to which you have added an apostrophe. Be careful not to add needless apostrophes. If the line is correct, write *C* in the blank.

EXAMPLE

Many poets have written about loves difficulties.   *love's*

1. George Merediths *Modern Love* is one of the famous   _____
   accounts of a couples marital problems.   _____
2. Its the nineteenth-centurys most interesting study of a _____
   husband and wifes relationship over a period of years.   _____
3. The poems organization is loose, but the subject matter _____
   justifies the disorganization.   _____
4. Meredith traces the progress of his own marriage, of its _____
   dissolution and eventual collapse.   _____
5. The causes of the man and womans marital discord are   _____
   presented along with the hopelessness that is theirs.   _____
6. Realizing that loves ardor has come and gone, the   _____
   couple pretend that alls well.   _____
7. At dinner parties their actions toward each other are so _____
   affectionate that their guests envy of their love is ap- _____
   parent.
8. Everyones impression is that his hosts relationship is   _____
   ideal.
9. The couple themselves enjoy and admire each others   _____
   pretension.
10. The poet doesnt fail to recognize the games true name, _____
    "Hiding the Skeleton."
11. When the guests have gone, the couples agony returns   _____
    because each must once again face his partners real   _____
    personality.
12. At night the man realizes that hes lost his wife, for her _____
    actions tell him that she loves another.   _____

83

13. The man finds one of his wifes letters to her lover, and he recalls that once she wrote similar words of love to him. _____

14. *Modern Love* reads like a modern psychologists analysis of a couple whose marriage is doomed to failure by their own mismatched personalities. _____

15. The poem exposes two peoples reactions to each other through alternating periods of hostility and attraction. _____

16. Many mens reaction to a beautiful woman would parallel the mans in the poem. _____

17. He cant resist his mates beauty even though he knows that theres no chance for them to be happy together. _____

18. He has followed Socrates advice in that he knows himself, but he cannot act upon what he knows. _____

19. The wife often displays what many people would consider a typical females behavior: she either cries or remains silent, regardless of her husbands efforts to communicate. _____

20. The poem is indeed modern in its perception of male and female behavior patterns even though it was published in the 1860s, when the poet was in his early twenties. _____

16

Use quotation marks to set off all direct quotations, some titles, and words used in a special sense. Place other marks of punctuation in proper relation to quotation marks.

16a   Use double quotation marks to enclose direct quotations.

Enclose all direct (but not indirect) quotations within double quotation marks (" "). Use single quotation marks (' ') for a quotation within another quotation. Remember that quotation marks must be used in pairs.

> "I feel," said Nan, "that the statement 'All men are created equal' is the cornerstone of liberty."
> She said, "Equality is a basic right."   [Direct quotation]
> She said that equality is a basic right.   [Indirect quotation]

Note: Long prose quotations and three or more lines of poetry are indented from the body of the text and single-spaced. Quotation marks are not used.

16b   Use quotation marks for minor titles.

Titles of short stories, articles from magazines, short poems, and chapters from books are regularly enclosed in quotation marks.

16c   Sometimes quotation marks enclose words used in a special sense.

> An eminent virologist has said that a "good" virus is hard to find.

16d   Do not overuse quotation marks.

> NEEDLESS PUNCTUATION   "Mike" will be here in a hour.

16e   Position quotation marks in relation to other marks of punctuation.

(1) The period and the comma are always placed *within* the quotation marks.

> "Play ball," the umpire shouted. "The rain is over."

(2) The colon and the semicolon are always placed *outside* the quotation marks.

> The test covered "Chicago"; next week we begin *Abraham Lincoln.*

(3) The dash, the question mark, and the exclamation point are placed within the quotation marks when they apply only to the quoted matter; they are placed outside when they apply to the whole sentence.

> He shouted, "Where are my record albums?"
> What is meant by "the generation gap"?

17

Use the period, the question mark, the exclamation point, the colon, the dash, parentheses, and brackets in accordance with accepted usage.

17a Use the period after declarative and mildly imperative sentences, after indirect questions, and after most abbreviations.

Jon fainted**.**   Come quickly**.**   Ask Dr**.** Oldham if he can come**.**

17b Use the question mark after direct (not after indirect) questions.

Did you hear my new record**?**   I asked if you heard my new record.

17c Use the exclamation point after emphatic interjections and after phrases, clauses, or sentences to express surprise or other strong emotion.

Horrors**!**   The car crashed**!**   How terrible**!**

17d Use the colon after a formal introductory statement to direct attention to what follows.

The famous passage reads**:**   [Here the colon introduces a long quotation. Commas are generally used to introduce a short quotation.]
There were three items on her grocery list**:** milk, eggs, and bacon. [Note that a dash may be used instead of the colon here.]

17e Use the dash to mark a sudden break in thought, to set off a summary, or to set off a parenthetical element that is very abrupt or that has commas within it.

Many dances of the 1960's——the twist, the frug, and the swim——emphasize the separation of the sexes.

17f Use parentheses (1) to enclose figures or letters when used for enumeration, as in this rule, and (2) to set off parenthetical, supplementary, or illustrative matter.

Parentheses set off parts loosely joined to the sentence and minimize them.

Bette **(**pronounced "Bet"**)** is an actress.

17g Use brackets to set off editorial comments in quoted matter.

One of Shakespeare's most famous lines is, "My **[**Macbeth's**]**   way of life / Is fall'n into the sere, the yellow leaf."

NAME _____ SCORE _____

DIRECTIONS   In the sentences below insert all needed quotation marks. In the blanks at the right enter these marks and the first and last word of each quoted part. Include other marks of punctuation used with the quotation marks, placed in their proper positions. Do not enclose indirect quotations. Write *C* in the blank at the right to indicate that a sentence is correct without quotation marks.

EXAMPLES

Many writers have said that woman is inferior to man.   *C*

Shakespeare wrote, "Frailty, thy name is woman."   *"Frailty — woman."*

1. What are some of the famous quotations about women? you ask.   _____

2. In *Don Juan* Byron said, In her first passion Woman loves her lover, / In all the others all she loves is love.   _____

3. Byron made one of the best-known comments on the love of women:

    Alas! the love of women! it is known
       To be a lovely and a fearful thing;
    For all of theirs upon that die is thrown,
       And if 'tis lost, Life hath no more to bring
    To them but mockeries of the past alone.   _____

4. Byron also said that the revenge of women who have been jilted is deadly and quick.   _____

5. But he went on, They are right; for Man, to man so oft unjust, / Is always so to women.   _____

6. In the article The Womanly Image, in the March, 1970, *Atlantic Monthly,* Paula Stern argues against the view of woman's love popularized by Byron.   _____

7. She says that when she sought a job, she was asked, Miss Stern, are you in love?   _____

8. Miss Stern claims that no man would be asked that question because his future is assumed to hold both a career and love.   _____

9. You may well question, Have any male writers spoken out against the stereotyping of woman as only wife and lover?

10. Henrik Ibsen, a nineteenth-century Norwegian playwright, had his female character in *A Doll's House* say to her husband: I believe that before all else I am a human being, just as much as you are—or at least that I should try to become one. . . . Henceforth I can't be satisfied with what most people say, and what is in books.

11. Here I have been your doll-wife, the woman tells her husband, just as at home I used to be papa's doll child. And the children, in their turn, have been my dolls.

12. That's a very noble speech, you may say, but what happened to a woman in the nineteenth century who had the courage to say to her husband, There must be perfect freedom on both sides?

13. The woman realized her plight when she said, I have no idea what will become of me.

14. In his notes for *A Doll's House,* Ibsen observed: A woman cannot be herself in the society of the present day, which is an exclusively masculine society.

15. John Stuart Mill, a nineteenth-century essayist, argued that women deserve the same privileges in society that men have.

16. I believe, Mill claimed, that their [women's] disabilities elsewhere are only clung to in order to maintain their subordination in domestic life; because the generality of the male sex cannot yet tolerate the idea of living with an equal.

Commas and other marks of punctuation

NAME _____ SCORE _____

DIRECTIONS In the sentences below insert all needed marks of punctuation. Also enter these marks in the same order in the blanks at the right. Be careful, both in the sentences and in the blanks at the right, to place quotation marks in proper relation to other marks of punctuation.

EXAMPLE

John Milton‚a seventeenth-century poet‚gave us in *Paradise Lost* one of literature's most famous depictions of man and woman.   *, ,* *literature's*

1. Milton who was married three times obviously had no great respect for the female sex his attitude being evidenced in several works.   _____ _____ _____

2. Milton's depiction of the first woman Eve indicates his opinion of womans failings.   _____ _____

3. Created to alleviate man's loneliness Eve eventually causes not only her own downfall but also Adams.   _____ _____

4. Soon after God has created her from the rib of Adam she shows what is to be her greatest weakness an overpowering vanity.   _____ _____

5. Convinced that Eve is the most beautiful of all creatures Adam tells the angel Raphael Yet when I approach / Her Eve's loveliness, . . . what she wills to do or say / Seems wisest, virtuousest, discreetest, best.   _____ _____ _____

6. Raphael warns Adam that man should not be misled by Eve's beauty that her outward fairness is not equal to man's inner wisdom.   _____ _____ _____

7. But Adam who promptly forgets Raphael's warning agrees to let Eve have her way when she argues that they should separate and work in different areas of the Garden of Eden.   _____ _____ _____

8. Satan who has observed Eve's vanity chooses to tempt the woman not the man because he claims the woman is intellectually inferior to the man.   _____ _____ _____

9. In the hope of becoming equal to Adam in intellect or one should really say superior to Adam Eve listens to the serpents offer.   _____ _____

10. She convinces herself that what the serpent says is true then she eats the forbidden fruit.

11. When she tells Adam what she has done he knows that she is doomed but he loves her so much that he cant live without her thus he chooses to eat the fruit and share his wife's fate.

12. A comparison of the motives of Adam and Eve reveals the obvious prejudice that Milton had against women Eve eats the fruit to become superior to Adam Adam eats the fruit to remain with Eve.

13. Love almost everyone will agree is a higher motive than pride the cause of woman's defeat.

14. In fact most Christian works such as *Paradise Lost* and *The Divine Comedy* depict pride as the most serious of all sins.

15. Pride according to Milton is the cause of Satan's fall from heaven it is also the cause of Adam and Eves loss of the Garden of Eden.

16. In *Samson Agonistes* a long verse drama Milton again indicts woman he has Delilah sell her husband to the enemy.

17. The beautiful vain Delilah convinces her husband to have his hair shorn an act that costs him his strength.

18. These are thy wonted arts, / And arts of every woman false like thee— Samson says To break all faith, all vows, deceive, betray.

19. Milton suggested through his female characters Eve and Delilah see the Bible for Milton's departures from his models that woman is proud selfish and deceitful.

20. Milton's male characters appear to have only one failing their love for women.

Review of all marks of punctuation

NAME _____ SCORE _____

DIRECTIONS   Use in sentences of your own, with proper capitalization and punctuation, each of the elements listed below. In the space at the right show all marks of punctuation used (except periods to end sentences).

EXAMPLE   a word, or words, in apposition

Milton's depiction of Eve, the first woman, is   '   ,   ,
the stereotype many people believe in.

1. two coordinate adjectives modifying the same noun (**12c**)   _____

2. a restrictive clause (**12d**)   _____

3. two main clauses not joined by a coordinating conjunction (**14a**)   _____

4. a series of three verbs (**12c**)   _____

5. a parenthetical phrase (**12d**)   _____

6. a direct question (**17b**)   _____

7. two main clauses joined by a coordinating conjunction (**12a**)   _____

8. a summary within a sentence (**17e**)   _____

9. an introductory adverbial clause (**12b**)   _____

10. a nonrestrictive clause (**12d**)   _____

11. a list of items at the end of a sentence (**17d**)   _____

12. a quotation interrupted by *he replied* (**12d**)   _____

DIRECTIONS Use in sentences of your own, with proper capitalization and punctuation, each of the elements listed below. Enter in the space at the right the specific word form, word, or title (properly punctuated) that you are required to use in the sentence.

EXAMPLE   the title of a long play

Edward Albee's "Who's Afraid of Virginia Woolf" presents a frightening game that some men and women play.

Who's Afraid of Virginia Woolf

13. a foreign word or phrase (**10**)

_____

14. the possessive of *who* (**15b**)

_____

15. the contraction of *who is* (**15c**)

_____

16. the possessive plural of *son-in-law* (**15a**)

_____

17. the possessive plural of *man* (**15a**)

_____

18. the title of a magazine article (**16b**)

_____

19. the title of a book (**10**)

_____

20. the title of a short poem (**16b**)

_____

Spelling and Hyphenation   sp 18

18

Spell every word according to established usage as shown by a good dictionary.

Mastering the words you misspell as they come to your attention day by day is undoubtedly one of the best methods of improving your spelling. This method, which was explained in the Preface, will be continued throughout the course. But you may get a special insight into your difficulties by analyzing the list of words you have misspelled. Once you have determined your particular difficulties, you may help to overcome them by learning to apply the rules designed to help you. You should certainly not burden yourself with those rules which, by analysis of your spelling, you find not applicable to your needs. As a basis for the exercises in this section, the common reasons for misspelling are listed below.

18a   Mispronunciation

(1) Do not omit a letter: *arctic, family, used*

(2) Do not add a letter: *athlete, film, hindrance*

(3) Do not change a letter: *accurate, prejudice*

(4) Do not transpose letters: *cavalry, hundred, prefer*

18b   Confusion of words similar in sound

Distinguish between words of similar sound and spelling.

   allusion, illusion; berth, birth; dual, duel; lose, loose

If your errors fall chiefly under **18a** and **18b**, you are not actually a poor speller; your misspellings are due to your insufficient knowledge of pronunciation and the exact meanings of words.

18c   Failure to distinguish prefix from root; changes in adding suffixes

(1) Add the prefix to the root without doubling or dropping letters.

   dis- (prefix) + appear (root) = disappear   [One *s*]
   im- + mortal = immortal   [Two *m*'s]
   un- + necessary = unnecessary   [Two *n*'s]

93

(2) Drop the final e before a suffix beginning with a vowel but not before a suffix beginning with a consonant.

> bride + -al = bridal; fame + -ous = famous
> care + -ful = careful; entire + -ly = entirely

Exceptions: *due, duly; awe, awful; hoe, hoeing; singe, singeing.* After *c* or *g* the final *e* is retained before suffixes beginning with *a* or *o: notice, notice-able; courage, courageous.*

(3) When the suffix begins with a vowel (-*ing*, -*ed*, -*ence*, -*ance*, -*able*), double a final single consonant if it is preceded by a single vowel and comes in an accented syllable. (A word of one syllable, of course, is always accented.)

> mop, mopping; run, running
> con·fer′, con·fer′red   [Final consonant in the accented syllable]
> ben′e·fit, ben′e·fited   [Final consonant not in the accented syllable]
> need, needed   [Final consonant not preceded by a single vowel]

Note how important this rule is in forming the present participle and the past tense of verbs.

(4) Except before -*ing*, final y preceded by a consonant is changed to *i* before a suffix.

> defy + -ance = defiance; happy + -ness = happiness
> modify + -er = modifier; modify + -ing = modifying

Final *y* preceded by a vowel is usually not changed before a suffix.

> annoy + -ed = annoyed; array + -ing = arraying

Exceptions: *pay, paid; lay, laid; say, said; day, daily.*

18d   Confusion of *ei* and *ie*

If you confuse these letters in your spelling, learn and follow these two rules: (1) When the sound is *ee* (as in *see*), write *ei* after *c* (*receipt, ceiling*) and *ie* after any other letter (*relieve, priest*). (2) When the sound is other than *ee*, usually write *ei: eight, their, reign.*

Exceptions: *either, neither, financier, leisure, seize, species, weird.*

18e   Forming the plural

Form the plural by adding *s* to the singular (*boy, boys*) but by adding *es* if the plural makes an extra syllable (*bush, bushes*).

18f   Hyphenated words

In general, use the hyphen **(1)** between words serving as a single adjective before a noun (a *know-it-all* expression), **(2)** with compound numbers from twenty-one to ninety-nine, **(3)** with prefixes or suffixes for clarity (*re-creation* of the scene), and **(4)** with the prefixes *ex-* (meaning "former"), *self-*, *all-*, and the adjective *-elect* (*mayor-elect*).

NAME _____ SCORE _____

DIRECTIONS Study as necessary the following words in groups of fifty (or as directed by your instructor) and use each word in a sentence (written out on a separate sheet of paper). Copy in your Individual Spelling List on pages 175–76 every word that you tend to misspell, following carefully the directions on page 175.

This spelling list is drawn from Dean Thomas Clark Pollock's study of 31,375 misspellings in the written work of college students.[1]

The Hundred Words Most Frequently Misspelled

In the list below the most troublesome letters for all words are in boldface. Asterisks indicate the most frequently misspelled words among the first hundred. Only American spellings are given.

[I]		[II]	
1. accommodate	26. embarrass	51. performance	76. repetition
2. achievement	27. environment	52. personal	77. rhythm
3. acquire	28. exaggerate	53. personnel	78. sense
4. all right	29. existence *	54. possession	79. separate *
5. among	30. existent *	55. possible	80. separation *
6. apparent	31. experience	56. practical	81. shining
7. argument	32. explanation	57. precede *	82. similar *
8. arguing	33. fascinate	58. prejudice	83. studying
9. belief *	34. height	59. prepare	84. succeed
10. believe *	35. interest	60. prevalent	85. succession
11. beneficial	36. its, it's	61. principal	86. surprise
12. benefited	37. led	62. principle	87. technique
13. category	38. lose	63. privilege *	88. than
14. coming	39. losing	64. probably	89. then
15. comparative	40. marriage	65. proceed	90. their *
16. conscious	41. mere	66. procedure	91. there *
17. controversy	42. necessary	67. professor	92. they're *
18. controversial	43. occasion *	68. profession	93. thorough
19. definitely	44. occurred	69. prominent	94. to, * too, * two *
20. definition	45. occurring	70. pursue	95. transferred
21. define	46. occurrence	71. quiet	96. unnecessary
22. describe	47. opinion	72. receive *	97. villain
23. description	48. opportunity	73. receiving *	98. woman
24. disastrous	49. paid	74. recommend	99. write
25. effect	50. particular	75. referring *	100. writing

The Next 550 Words Most Frequently Misspelled

[III]	102. abundance	104. academic	106. academy
101. absence	103. abundant	105. academically	107. acceptable

---

[1] Thomas Clark Pollock and William D. Baker, *The University Spelling Book* (Englewood Cliffs, N.J.: Prentice-Hall, 1955), pp. 6–12. See also Thomas Clark Pollock, "Spelling Report," *College English*, 16 (Nov. 1954), 102–09.

108. acceptance
109. accepting
110. accessible
111. accidental
112. accidentally
113. acclaim
114. accompanied
115. accompanies
116. accompaniment
117. accompanying
118. accomplish
119. accuracy
120. accurate
121. accurately
122. accuser
123. accuses
124. accusing
125. accustom
126. acquaintance
127. across
128. actuality
129. actually
130. adequately
131. admission
132. admittance
133. adolescence
134. adolescent
135. advantageous
136. advertisement
137. advertiser
138. advertising
139. advice, advise
140. affect
141. afraid
142. against
143. aggravate
144. aggressive
145. alleviate
146. allotted
147. allotment
148. allowed
149. allows
150. already

[IV]
151. altar
152. all together

153. altogether
154. amateur
155. amount
156. analysis
157. analyze
158. and
159. another
160. annually
161. anticipated
162. apologetically
163. apologized
164. apology
165. apparatus
166. appearance
167. applies
168. applying
169. appreciate
170. appreciation
171. approaches
172. appropriate
173. approximate
174. area
175. arise
176. arising
177. arouse
178. arousing
179. arrangement
180. article
181. atheist
182. athlete
183. athletic
184. attack
185. attempts
186. attendance
187. attendant
188. attended
189. attitude
190. audience
191. authoritative
192. authority
193. available
194. bargain
195. basically
196. basis
197. beauteous
198. beautified
199. beautiful

200. beauty

[V]
201. become
202. becoming
203. before
204. began
205. beginner
206. beginning
207. behavior
208. bigger
209. biggest
210. boundary
211. breath
212. breathe
213. brilliance
214. brilliant
215. Britain
216. Britannica
217. burial
218. buried
219. bury
220. business
221. busy
222. calendar
223. capitalism
224. career
225. careful
226. careless
227. carried
228. carrier
229. carries
230. carrying
231. cemetery
232. certainly
233. challenge
234. changeable
235. changing
236. characteristic
237. characterized
238. chief
239. children
240. Christian
241. Christianity
242. choice
243. choose
244. chose

245. cigarette
246. cite
247. clothes
248. commercial
249. commission
250. committee

[VI]
251. communist
252. companies
253. compatible
254. competition
255. competitive
256. competitor
257. completely
258. concede
259. conceivable
260. conceive
261. concentrate
262. concern
263. condemn
264. confuse
265. confusion
266. connotation
267. connote
268. conscience
269. conscientious
270. consequently
271. considerably
272. consistency
273. consistent
274. contemporary
275. continuously
276. controlled
277. controlling
278. convenience
279. convenient
280. correlate
281. council
282. counselor
283. countries
284. create
285. criticism
286. criticize
287. cruelly
288. cruelty
289. curiosity

290. curious	335. endeavor	380. generally	425. indispensable
291. curriculum	336. enjoy	381. genius	426. individually
292. dealt	337. enough	382. government	427. industries
293. deceive	338. enterprise	383. governor	428. inevitable
294. decided	339. entertain	384. grammar	429. influence
295. decision	340. entertainment	385. grammatically	430. influential
296. dependent	341. entirely	386. group	431. ingenious
297. desirability	342. entrance	387. guaranteed	432. ingredient
298. desire	343. equipment	388. guidance	433. initiative
299. despair	344. equipped	389. guiding	434. intellect
300. destruction	345. escapade	390. handled	435. intelligence
	346. escape	391. happened	436. intelligent
[VII]	347. especially	392. happiness	437. interference
301. detriment	348. etc.	393. hear	438. interpretation
302. devastating	349. everything	394. here	439. interrupt
303. device, devise	350. evidently	395. heroes	440. involve
304. difference		396. heroic	441. irrelevant
305. different	[VIII]	397. heroine	442. irresistible
306. difficult	351. excellence	398. hindrance	443. irritable
307. dilemma	352. excellent	399. hopeless	444. jealousy
308. diligence	353. except	400. hoping	445. knowledge
309. dining	354. excitable		446. laboratory
310. disappoint	355. exercise	[IX]	447. laborer
311. disciple	356. expense	401. hospitalization	448. laboriously
312. discipline	357. experiment	402. huge	449. laid
313. discrimination	358. extremely	403. humorist	450. later
314. discussion	359. fallacy	404. humorous	
315. disease	360. familiar	405. hundred	[X]
316. disgusted	361. families	406. hunger	451. leisurely
317. disillusioned	362. fantasies	407. hungrily	452. lengthening
318. dissatisfied	363. fantasy	408. hungry	453. license
319. divide	364. fashions	409. hypocrisy	454. likelihood
320. divine	365. favorite	410. hypocrite	455. likely
321. doesn't	366. fictitious	411. ideally	456. likeness
322. dominant	367. field	412. ignorance	457. listener
323. dropped	368. finally	413. ignorant	458. literary
324. due	369. financially	414. imaginary	459. literature
325. during	370. financier	415. imagination	460. liveliest
326. eager	371. foreigners	416. imagine	461. livelihood
327. easily	372. forty	417. immediately	462. liveliness
328. efficiency	373. forward	418. immense	463. lives
329. efficient	374. fourth	419. importance	464. loneliness
330. eighth	375. friendliness	420. incidentally	465. lonely
331. eliminate	376. fulfill	421. increase	466. loose
332. emperor	377. fundamentally	422. indefinite	467. loss
333. emphasize	378. further	423. independence	468. luxury
334. encourage	379. gaiety	424. independent	469. magazine

470. magnificence	515. parliament	560. religion	605. sufficient
471. magnificent	516. paralyzed	561. remember	606. summary
472. maintenance	517. passed	562. reminisce	607. summed
473. management	518. past	563. represent	608. suppose
474. maneuver	519. peace	564. resources	609. suppress
475. manner	520. peculiar	565. response	610. surrounding
476. manufacturers	521. perceive	566. revealed	611. susceptible
477. material	522. permanent	567. ridicule	612. suspense
478. mathematics	523. permit	568. ridiculous	613. swimming
479. matter	524. persistent	569. roommate	614. symbol
480. maybe	525. persuade	570. sacrifice	615. synonymous
481. meant	526. pertain	571. safety	616. temperament
482. mechanics	527. phase	572. satire	617. tendency
483. medical	528. phenomenon	573. satisfied	618. themselves
484. medicine	529. philosophy	574. satisfy	619. theories
485. medieval	530. physical	575. scene	620. theory
486. melancholy	531. piece	576. schedule	621. therefore
487. methods	532. planned	577. seize	622. those
488. miniature	533. plausible	578. sentence	623. thought
489. minutes	534. playwright	579. sergeant	624. together
490. mischief	535. pleasant	580. several	625. tomorrow
491. moral	536. politician	581. shepherd	626. tragedy
492. morale	537. political	582. significance	627. tremendous
493. morally	538. practice	583. simile	628. tried
494. mysterious	539. predominant	584. simple	629. tries
495. narrative	540. preferred	585. simply	630. tyranny
496. naturally	541. presence	586. since	631. undoubtedly
497. Negroes	542. prestige	587. sincerely	632. unusually
498. ninety	543. primitive	588. sociology	633. useful
499. noble	544. prisoners	589. sophomore	634. useless
500. noticeable	545. propaganda	590. source	635. using
	546. propagate	591. speaking	636. vacuum
[XI]	547. prophecy	592. speech	637. valuable
501. noticing	548. psychoanalysis	593. sponsor	638. varies
502. numerous	549. psychology	594. stabilization	639. various
503. obstacle	550. psychopathic	595. stepped	640. view
504. off		596. stories	641. vengeance
505. omit	[XII]	597. story	642. warrant
506. operate	551. psychosomatic	598. straight	643. weather
507. oppose	552. quantity	599. strength	644. weird
508. opponent	553. really	600. stretch	645. where
509. opposite	554. realize		646. whether
510. optimism	555. rebel	[XIII]	647. whole
511. organization	556. recognize	601. strict	648. whose
512. original	557. regard	602. stubborn	649. yield
513. pamphlets	558. relative	603. substantial	650. you're
514. parallel	559. relieve	604. subtle	

NAME _____ SCORE _____

DIRECTIONS   With the aid of your dictionary write out each of the following words by syllables, mark the position of the main accent, and pronounce the word correctly and distinctly. In your pronunciation avoid any careless omission, addition, change, or transposition.

EXAMPLE   candidate *can′di·date*

1. hungry _____

2. mischievous _____

3. suffrage _____

4. surprise _____

5. perspiration _____

6. column _____

7. vacuum _____

8. escape _____

9. miniature _____

10. environment _____

11. chocolate _____

12. grievous _____

13. library _____

14. temperature _____

15. probably _____

16. lengthening _____

17. equipment _____

18. boundary _____

19. hurrying _____

20. laboratory _____

21. prepare _____

22. acceptance _____

23. ridiculous _____

24. quantity _____

25. participate _____

26. incidentally _____

27. children _____

28. hindrance _____

29. mathematics _____

30. despair _____

NAME _____ SCORE _____

DIRECTIONS In the following sentences strike out the spelling or spellings within parentheses that do not fit the meaning and write the correct spelling in the blank at the right. Consult your dictionary freely.

EXAMPLE

What (role, ~~roll~~) should women play today? *role*

1. (Their, There, They're) are many questions to be an-
swered about (who's, whose) to blame for sexual stereotyping. _____

2. One person (beliefs, believes) that writers like Milton
are to blame whereas another (cites, sights, sites) historical evidence. _____

3. Some people are still (quiet, quite) convinced that biological make-up establishes the (coarse, course) of behavior for each sex. _____

4. Certainly no one is likely to (loose, lose) interest in the
battle between the sexes regardless of the opinion he
(accepts, excepts). _____

5. The (affect, effect) of feminism is only beginning to be
felt in society; women's liberation will be a (relevant,
reverent) issue for many years to come. _____

6. A great deal has happened in the (passed, past) twenty
years to cause people to (altar, alter) their attitude
about both woman's and man's place in society. _____

7. (Weather, Whether) or not one subscribes to the feminists' position, he must recognize that their movement
has had an (affect, effect) on male as well as female
behavior. _____

8. It is (to, too, two) early for us to make a (thorough,
through) analysis of the feminist movement. _____

9. But we can observe many changes in behavior patterns
that feminism has (lead, led) to, and we can safely
(prophecy, prophesy) many more to come. _____

10. One of the (principal, principle) earmarks of our age
has been a (braking, breaking) away from tradition. _____

NAME _____ SCORE _____

DIRECTIONS In the blank at the right enter the correct spelling of each word with suffix added. In the middle blank state the reason for the spelling entered.

EXAMPLE

come + -ing *Drop final e before a vowel.* *coming*

1. arrange + -ing _____ _____

2. arrange + -ment _____ _____

3. awe + -ful _____ _____

4. advantage + -ous _____ _____

5. lop + -ing _____ _____

6. prefer + -ed _____ _____

7. loop + -ing _____ _____

8. admit + -ance _____ _____

9. leap + -ing _____ _____

10. carry + -ed _____ _____

11. carry + -ing _____ _____

12. hope + -ing _____ _____

13. hope + -ful _____ _____

14. destroy + -ed _____ _____

NAME _____ SCORE _____

DIRECTIONS   With the aid of your dictionary fill in the blanks in the following words by writing *ei* or *ie*. In the blank preceding the word state the rule applicable. Write *Exception* in the blank preceding any word that is an exception to the rule.

EXAMPLE

When the sound is ee, write ei after c.   dec*ei*ve

1. _____ ach___ve

2. _____ for___gn

3. _____ perc___ve

4. _____ f___ld

5. _____ w___rd

6. _____ gr___f

7. _____ w___ght

8. _____ pr___st

9. _____ v___n

10. _____ p___rce

11. _____ d___gn

12. _____ y___ld

13. _____ w___ld

14. _____ s___ne

15. _____ sl___gh

16. _____ sh___ld

17. _____ conc___t

18. _____ ch___f

19. _____ spec___s

20. _____ med___val

19

Learn how to use the dictionary; select appropriate words.

One of the best investments a student makes is the purchase of a good desk dictionary. Unabridged dictionaries, like *Webster's Third New International,* can be found in the library, but everyday use requires a smaller, abridged dictionary. A desk dictionary is used for more purposes than finding the correct spelling of a word. To name only a few others, it tells the student how to pronounce a word like *harass;* what a word like *fancy* originally meant, as well as the various meanings it has today; what the principal parts for an irregular verb like *sing* are; and what usage label may be given for a word like *poke.*

Dictionaries vary in their listing of usage labels; some, in fact, have dropped most labels. Once the student has secured a good desk dictionary, he should study the introductory matter to learn the attitude his dictionary takes toward usage labels as well as the order in which the meanings of words are listed—that is, in order of historical development or of common usage.

19a Using the dictionary intelligently Most words (or meanings of words) in the dictionary are unlabeled—that is, they have no label such as *Slang* or *Dialectal* and are accordingly in good and general use throughout the English-speaking world. Unlabeled words (or unlabeled meanings of words) make up what is called the standard or formal English vocabulary and may be used freely as they fit the writer's needs. But words entered in the dictionary with a label should be used with caution.

19b Informal words Informal words (labeled *Informal* or *Colloquial* by most dictionaries) are appropriate to the conversation of cultivated people and to informal writing but tend to bring a discordant note into formal writing.

INFORMAL   I played hooky, but I didn't get away with it.
FORMAL   I stayed away from school, but I was discovered.

19c Slang Slang is a special type of colloquial language that is often objectionable because it tends to become trite and vague.

SLANG   This is a *crummy* apartment.
STANDARD   This is a *shabby* (OR *inferior*) apartment.

19d Dialectal words Dialectal words (labeled *Dialectal* or assigned to some locality, such as *Southern U.S.*) should normally be avoided because they are often meaningless outside the limited region where they are current.

DIALECTAL   It was *boughten.*
STANDARD   It was *not homemade.*   OR   It was *bought at the store.*

19e   Vulgarisms or illiteracies   Vulgarisms (labeled *Illiterate*) are the nonstandard expressions of uneducated people and are usually not listed in the dictionary.

NONSTANDARD   *They's* no one here but me.
STANDARD   *There's* no one here but me.

19f   Obsolete or archaic words   Obsolete words are no longer in general use, but they are listed as an aid in reading our older literature.

19g   Technical words   Technical words (given such labels as *Law, Architecture, Nautical*) are peculiar to one group or profession and should be avoided in addressing a general audience or in writing for the general reader.

20

Find the exact, idiomatic, fresh word.

WRONG WORD   The explosion *effected* her hearing.
RIGHT WORD   The explosion *affected* her hearing.
UNIDIOMATIC   It was a difficult task he *set to* me.
IDIOMATIC   It was a difficult task he *set for* me.
TRITE   This is *a shining example of* good writing.
BETTER   This is good writing *at its best.*

21

Avoid wordiness.

WORDY   The reason why I dread the summer is because my room is hot.
BETTER   I dread the summer because my room is hot.
REPETITIOUS   There are *various and sundry* theories about education.
BETTER   There are *various* theories about education.

22

Omit no word essential to the meaning.

INCOMPLETE   The French class is over and the students leaving.
COMPLETE   The French class is over and the students *are* leaving.

NAME _____ SCORE _____

The full title, the edition, and the date of publication of my dictionary are as follows:

_____

1. Abbreviations   Where are abbreviations found? _____
Write out the meaning of each of the abbreviations following these sample entries:

gain, *v.t., OFr.* _____   oft, *adv., Goth.* _____

martial, *adj., L.* _____   or, *conj.* _____

2. Spelling and Pronunciation   Write out by syllables each of the words listed below and place the accent where it belongs. Consult your dictionary. With the aid of the diacritical marks (in parentheses immediately after the word) and the key at the bottom of the page or in the introductory matter, determine the preferred pronunciation (the first pronunciation given) of each word. Then pronounce each word correctly several times. Be prepared to pronounce each word in class.

execrable _____   advertisement _____

obsequious _____   exquisite _____

Write the plurals of the following words:

memory _____ spoonful _____ spouse _____ knife _____

Determine which of the following words should be written with a hyphen and rewrite those that need a hyphen.

makeup _____ straightforward _____ shortlived _____

3. Derivations   The derivation, or origin, of a word (given in brackets) often furnishes a literal meaning that throws much light on the word. For each of the following words give (a) the source—the language from which it is derived, (b) the original word or words, and (c) the original meaning.

	Source	*Original Word and Meaning*
sympathy	_____	_____
interlude	_____	_____
affront	_____	_____

4. Meanings   Usually words develop several different meanings. (Note that *Webster's Seventh New Collegiate Dictionary* and *Webster's New World*

Dictionary of the American Language list meanings 1, 2, etc., in order of historical development.) How many meanings are listed for the following words?

discuss, *v.t.* _____   distance, *n.* _____   distant, *adj.* _____

distaff, *n.* _____   distance, *v.t.* _____   over, *prep.* _____

5. Special Labels   Words (or certain meanings of words) may have such precautionary or explanatory labels as *Archaic, Colloquial, Dialectal, Obsolete, Slang, Nautical,* or *Law.* What label or special usage do you find for one meaning of each of the following words?

pooch, *n.* _____   damsel, *n.* _____   dander, *n.* _____

gate, *v.t.* _____   gang, *v.t.* _____   fix, *v.i.* _____

6. Synonyms   Even among words with nearly the same essential meaning, one word usually fits a given sentence more exactly than any other. To show exact shades of meaning, some dictionaries treat in special paragraphs certain groups of closely related words. What synonyms are specially differentiated in your dictionary along with the following words?

introduce, *v.t.* _____

importance, *n.* _____

7. Capitalization   Of the following words rewrite those that should be capitalized.

democracy _____   freudian _____   english _____

indian _____   summer _____   history _____

8. Grammatical Information   Note that many words may serve as two or more parts of speech. Classify each of the following words (according to the first listing in the dictionary) as *v.i., v.t., n., adj., prep.,* or *conj.* Give the principal parts of each verb.

high _____   kill _____   once _____

into _____   run _____   if _____

9. Miscellaneous Information   Answer the following questions by referring to your dictionary and be prepared to tell in what part of the dictionary the information is located.

In what century did Henry VIII rule? _____

Who was George Bernard Shaw? _____

What is the area of Cuba? _____

NAME _____ SCORE _____

DIRECTIONS   Consult your dictionary to determine whether the italicized words, as used in the following sentences, conform to formal English usage. If the word (or words), with the meaning it has in its particular sentence, is labeled in any way, enter this label (such as *Informal* or *Slang*) in the blank at the right. If the word is not labeled, write *Formal* in the blank. Go over your answers in class to compare the usage labels of various dictionaries.

EXAMPLE

There are *lots of* modern writers who have commented on   *Colloquial*
  male-female relationships.

1. D. H. Lawrence was a famous *chap* from England who   _____
   writ a great deal about male-female relationships.   _____

2. In "Odour of Chrysanthemums" Lawrence *allows* that   _____
   men and women have *plenty* trouble relating to each   _____
   other.

3. While the wife in the story *sets* around assuming her   _____
   husband is getting *tight* at the local bar, he is really   _____
   being *done in* by asphyxiation in the mine.   _____

4. Finally her husband's corpse is carried home, and she
   begins to *suspicion* for the first time the kind of rela-   _____
   tionship they have had for all their *marital* years.   _____

5. Despite their having *raised* two children for several   _____
   years and their having begun the life of a third, they
   have been in a miserable *fix* in their relationship to   _____
   each other.

6. The wife realizes that she has never really *kenned* her   _____
   husband; he has been a stranger to her *irregardless* of   _____
   their physical intimacy.

7. In death he is *inviolable,* and the woman cannot keep   _____
   from feeling *despite* for him.   _____

8. *E'en* though she feels something other than grief, she   _____
   tries to show sorrow for the death of the man *which*   _____
   has been her husband for many years.

9. As she prepares her husband's body for *laying out,* she   _____
   smells the odor of dead chrysanthemums in the room.

10. She remembers the times *afore* that she associated   _____
    with chrysanthemums—her wedding day, the birth of
    her daughter, and the first time her husband was
    brought home *pickled.*   _____

NAME _____ SCORE _____

DIRECTIONS   In the following sentences cross out any word or phrase not appropriate in formal writing. In the blank at the right enter the formal English equivalent. Write *C* in the blank opposite each sentence in which all words are used in accordance with formal writing.

EXAMPLE

The woman in "Odour of Chrysanthemums" ~~can't~~ hardly accept what she knows is true.   *can*

1. The woman cannot get her husband off of her mind.   _____

2. She knows that he went in the mine each day regretting his role as a husband.   _____

3. Being as he was the husband, his life's pattern was set.   _____

4. She realizes now that he is dead how different he was to the man she had thought him to be.   _____

5. She could of accepted him for what he was, but she had refused.   _____

6. She and he were two people which had lived together as strangers.   _____

7. Everything had seemed alright between them.   _____

8. But now she can see that they had not shared nothing.   _____

9. Regardless of the closeness of their bodies, they never really touched each other.   _____

10. "Odour of Chrysanthemums" does not suggest that a wife is inferior than her husband or vice versa, but it does imply that husbands and wives never really know each other.   _____

11. D. H. Lawrence had no doubt but what men and women have trouble relating to each other.   _____

12. Both the men and women in Lawrence's stories usually feel bad about their inability to understand each other.   _____

13. Most all Lawrence's female characters are materialistic.   _____

14. The male characters try and satisfy their mates' desire for security.   _____

15. Usually, though, the women want that they should have more money than their husbands can supply.   _____

NAME _____ SCORE _____

DIRECTIONS   Cross out the inappropriate word or words. Let the correct, exact word stand in the sentence and enter it in the space at the right. Consult your dictionary freely.

EXAMPLE

The (~~amount,~~ number) of stories that treat lack of communication in marriage is astounding.   _number_

1. Twentieth-century fiction seems to (imply, infer) that lack of communication is the primary difficulty of modern marriages.   _____

2. In James Joyce's "The Dead" the (perspective, prospective) of time reveals the true nature of a husband and wife's relationship.   _____

3. The husband has suffered from the (allusion, delusion) that his wife has always been totally devoted to him.   _____

4. He feels that he is (conscience, conscious) of all her thoughts and feelings.   _____

5. He is sure that he knows (everyone, every one) of her memories.   _____

6. Then one night he is surprised that an old love ballad can (elicit, illicit) a response from his wife.   _____

7. She becomes nostalgic as she (remonstrates, reminisces) about a past romantic experience.   _____

8. Her attention is completely (averted, diverted) from her husband's conversation.   _____

9. At first the husband is (incredible, incredulous) that his wife could have ever been romantically inclined toward anyone but himself.   _____

10. The husband (attributes, contributes) his wife's nostalgia to the snowy evening.   _____

11. Then the wife tells her husband about an important (incidence, incident) in the life of Michael Furey, a young boy who had once loved her.   _____

12. In spite of the (advice, advise) of his doctor, Michael had stood outside her window in the rain trying to speak with her.   _____

13. Michael had died a week later, his death perhaps the (affect, effect) of braving a storm to see his love.   _____

14. In comparison with Michael Furey's love, the husband feels his own is (contemptible, contemptuous).   _____

15. At this (instance, instant) many years later, Michael Furey is more alive for his wife than he is.   _____

16. In the years (preceding, proceeding) he had felt confident of his relationship with his wife.   _____

17. But now he realizes that he has never really known his wife, for she has kept the (image, imagery) of Michael Furey locked in her mind for all the years of their marriage.   _____

18. He knows that he must now (adapt, adopt) a new attitude toward his relationship with his wife.   _____

19. He realizes that their (marital, martial) relationship has not been what he imagined it to be.   _____

20. He becomes (cogitative, cognitive) of the fact that he and his wife have been living together as strangers.   _____

DIRECTIONS   Bracket needless words in each of the following sentences. For each sentence needing no further revision, write *1* in the blank at the right; for other sentences write *2* in the blank and make the needed revision.

EXAMPLES

James Thurber[was a man who] wrote humorous essays and stories about male-female relationships.   _____1_____

One character [by Thurber who is especially memorable] is the *especially memorable Thurber* ^ henpecked Walter Mitty.   _____2_____

1. In the story "The Secret World of Walter Mitty" it relates the dreams of the title character.   _____

2. In order that he might escape the constant bickering of his wife, Walter Mitty retreats to safety in a dream world.   _____

3. Mrs. Mitty thinks that her husband is worthless, and she does not have much regard for him.   _____

4. It is because of his wife's lack of respect for him that causes Walter to daydream about a better life.   _____

5. While Mrs. Mitty lectures him constantly and without stopping, Walter dreams that he is the brave commander of a ship.   _____

6. Walter not only dreams that he is a commander, but he also dreams that he is a famous surgeon and a daredevil pilot.   _____

7. Due to the fact that Mrs. Mitty cannot enter his dream world, Walter achieves a kind of victory over her.   _____

8. In the various and sundry stories that Thurber wrote, men and women are usually pitted against each other.   _____

9. "A Unicorn in the Garden" is another Thurber story, and it is one that shows a man and woman in conflict.   _____

10. The husband in the story is a man who is dominated by his wife.   _____

11. One day he finds a unicorn in his garden, and he enthusiastically reports that he has found a unicorn to his wife. _____

12. She talks to her husband and tells him that there is no such animal as a unicorn. _____

13. The husband is undaunted by his wife's skepticism, and he is not dismayed by it. _____

14. Typically the wife continues to make fun of her husband as she usually does. _____

15. The husband sees the unicorn again, and it is the second time when the wife decides to take drastic action. _____

16. She calls the police and tells the police to come immediately with a strait jacket for her husband. _____

17. She assures the police that her husband is insane on account of the fact that he claims to have seen a unicorn. _____

18. Unexpectedly the husband turns the tables on his wife and makes her seem to be the insane one when he tells the police that he has naturally never seen a unicorn because such an animal does not exist. _____

19. The police return back to headquarters with the wife, not the husband, in the strait jacket. _____

20. Thurber was an American writer, and he often depicted the eternal struggle between the sexes. _____

Omission of necessary words

NAME _____ SCORE _____

DIRECTIONS   In the following sentences insert the words that are needed to complete the sense and write these words in the blanks at the right.

EXAMPLE

Thurber was as famous as an essayist as *he was as* a short story writer.   *he was as*

1. Thurber wrote not only stories but essays about the war between the sexes.   _____

2. In "Courtship Through the Ages" Thurber implies that human beings have and always will practice strange behavior in courtship.   _____

3. Thurber was interested and skillful at describing animal behavior that is like human behavior.   _____

4. The courtship of man is not very different from an animal, Thurber suggests in "Courtship Through the Ages."   _____

5. In each example of animal courtship Thurber shows the male is eternally trying to please the female.   _____

6. The male may be as beautiful or even more beautiful than the peacock, but the female is not impressed.   _____

7. Perhaps the male fiddler crab makes a greater effort than any animal to attract a female.   _____

8. He stands on tiptoe all day long waving his large pincer in the air in the hope he might attract a female's attention.   _____

9. The male fiddler's efforts are as wasted as the peacock for the female of each species rarely responds to the male's presence.   _____

10. Thurber suggests the things the female animal notices are gifts.   _____

11. Thus the male has and always will be trapped into taking gifts to win the female's approval. _____

12. The bowerbird is a good example of the lengths which a male must go to please a female. _____

13. The female expects the male to construct a playground for her and put all kinds of things into it. _____

14. Through an example like the bowerbird Thurber is hinting the female of the human species expects the male to spare no effort to please her. _____

15. Each type male insect that Thurber discusses must literally make a fool of himself to win the female's approval. _____

16. During spring the female may be interested in love but only if the poor male presents her with acceptable gifts. _____

Unity and Logical Thinking   u 23

23

Bring into the sentence only related ideas and pertinent details. Complete each thought logically.

23a   Unrelated ideas should be developed in separate sentences.

If ideas are related, they should be expressed in such a way that the relationship is immediately clear to the reader.

UNRELATED   Mr. Jones serves on the school board, and he is an engineer.
IMPROVED   Mr. Jones serves on the school board. He is an engineer.   OR
Mr. Jones, an engineer, serves on the school board. [Unity secured by subordination of one idea]

23b   Excessive detail should not be allowed to obscure the central thought of the sentence.

Such detail, if important, should be developed in separate sentences; otherwise it should be omitted.

OVERLOADED   When I was just a child, living in my parents' house, which burned down long ago, I had already read most of the novels in the public library, which was close by.
BETTER   When I was just a child, I had already read most of the novels in the nearby public library. [If the writer considers other details important, he may add them in a second sentence: "I was then living in my parents' home, which burned down long ago."]

23c   Mixed, obscure, or illogical constructions should be avoided.

MIXED   This uprising must be reined in or it will boil over. [Figure of a spirited horse being controlled plus figure of liquid becoming overheated]
BETTER   This uprising must be reined in or it will get out of control. [Figure of a spirited horse carried throughout]
MIXED   Because he was ambitious caused him to leave the town. [An adverb clause, a part of a complex sentence, is here used as the subject of a simple sentence.]
CLEAR   His ambition caused him to leave the town. [Single sentence]   OR
Because he was ambitious he left the town. [Adverb clause retained; main clause added to complete the complex sentence]

115

MIXED	A hypocrite is when a person is insincere. [Avoid the *is when* or *is where* construction. A *when* clause, used as an adverb, cannot be substituted for a noun.]
LOGICAL	A hypocrite is an insincere person.
MIXED	To ostracize is where a person is excluded from a group. [Adverb clause misused as a noun]
LOGICAL	To ostracize a person is to exclude him from a group.
ILLOGICAL	She wouldn't hardly say a word. [Double negative]
LOGICAL	She would hardly say a word.

Subordination   sub 24

24

Use subordination to relate ideas concisely and effectively; use coordination only to give ideas equal emphasis.

24a   In general a related series of short, choppy sentences should be combined into longer units in which the lesser ideas are properly subordinated.

| CHOPPY | The Australian kangaroo is a marsupial. He can move at thirty miles an hour and clear most fences with ease. |
| BETTER | The Australian kangaroo, a marsupial, can move at thirty miles an hour and clear most fences with ease. |

24b   Two or more main clauses should not be carelessly joined by *and, so,* or other coordinating words when one clause should be subordinated to another.

Coordination should be used only for ideas of equal importance.

INEFFECTIVE	My car brakes failed and (OR SO) I had a wreck. [Two main clauses]
BETTER	Because my car brakes failed, I had a wreck.
ACCEPTABLE	The movie was good, but I did not enjoy it. [Coordination used to stress equally the movie and the reaction]
USUALLY BETTER	Although the movie was good, I did not enjoy it. [Stress on one of the two ideas—the reaction]

24c   Avoid illogical as well as awkward subordination.

| ABSURD | When the ball hit me, I leaned out the window. |
| LOGICAL | When I leaned out the window, the ball hit me. OR   The ball hit me when I leaned out the window. |

NAME _____ SCORE _____

DIRECTIONS   In the blank at the right of each of the following sentences enter *1, 2,* or *3* to indicate whether the chief difficulty is (1) joining of unrelated ideas, (2) use of excessive detail, or (3) mixed, obscure, or illogical construction. Then rewrite the sentences to make them effective.

EXAMPLE

Anthropology is ~~where one studies~~ *the study of the* characteristics of mankind.   *3*

1. When one studies primitive societies is a good way to learn about basic differences in the sexes.   _____

2. Margaret Mead is a famous anthropologist, and we learn a great deal from her books and articles about the differences in male and female behavior in various primitive societies.   _____

3. One of her books, *Male and Female,* which was published in 1949, presents a study based on her many years of anthropological research in South Pacific societies of the two sexes, both in America and elsewhere, in today's changing world, which offers new patterns of behavior to both male and female.   _____

4. Her study adds fuel to the argument that male and female psychologies are different.   _____

5. Because all societies set up different patterns of behavior for males and females is why Margaret Mead argues for an acceptance of basic differences in the abilities of the two sexes.   _____

6. One can't hardly say that a particular ability is always assigned to the male or to the female.   _____

7. In some societies men carry the heavy burdens, while in other societies women bear the burdens on their head.   _____

8. Thus women are considered weaker than men in some societies and stronger than men in others, and today women may become scientists, business executives, and politicians.   _____

9. In spite of the popular conception that parents worry only about marrying off their girls, who must often have dowries paid for them and who thus seem to be hardships for their parents, in some societies it is the boys, not the girls, whom the parents, naturally concerned about their offsprings' happiness, are troubled about marrying off. _____

10. Another surprising belief in some societies is when the male is designated as the vulnerable sex, the one in need of protection. _____

11. Thus in certain parts of the world the wives must protect their husband from harm. _____

12. No one character trait has never been found always to be associated with one sex. _____

13. While a given characteristic such as strength may be assigned to the male or female by one society and the opposite trait assigned by another society, Margaret Mead, the author of such books as *Male and Female* and *Coming of Age in Samoa*, points out that no society, regardless of how primitive or sophisticated it may be, assumes that the two sexes have the same physical and mental qualities except for the differences in reproductive organs. _____

14. Margaret Mead views the one-sex notion as a strike against the forward movement of civilization. _____

15. She feels that the cultural richness of any society is mainly because the two sexes are regarded as quite different. _____

16. She does think, however, that our society has tended to focus attention on the male's analytical ability and to by-pass the female's intuitive power. _____

Subordination for effectiveness

NAME _____ SCORE _____

DIRECTIONS   Combine each of the following groups of short sentences into one effective sentence. Express the most important idea in the main clause and put lesser ideas in subordinate clauses, phrases, or words. Use coordination only for ideas of equal importance.

EXAMPLE

There are many differences between the American marriage ideal and that of other societies. Margaret Mead discusses these differences. She discusses them in her book *Male and Female*.

In her book Male and Female Margaret Mead discusses the many differences between the American marriage ideal and that of other societies.

1. Margaret Mead claims that there is no more difficult marriage form than that found in the United States. She bases this opinion on the almost impossible predicament of the couple to be married. The couple attempt to have a successful marriage without the aid of their parents or society.

_____

_____

_____

_____

2. In many societies the parents arrange the marriage for the boy and girl. In America the boy and girl are supposed to marry without the help of their parents. Their parents may even disapprove of the marriage. In this case the boy and girl are expected to marry anyway if they really love each other.

_____

_____

_____

_____

3. The American marriage ideal is intrinsically contradictory. The boy and girl are supposed to choose each other from an unlimited number of possibilities. They are supposed to choose each other only on the basis of romantic love. Yet they are still expected to have the same general interests, personalities, and abilities.

_____

_____

_____

_____

4. The recognition of the equality of the female has led the boy to expect perfect companionship in marriage. He must choose an almost identical person to himself to have companionship. He must still pretend to be choosing only on the basis of romantic love.

_____

_____

_____

_____

5. Logically the boy would marry a girl from his own home town. The girl would be one whom he had known most of his life. In America the independent boy is expected to leave his familiar surroundings. He is supposed to look for a mate elsewhere.

_____

_____

_____

_____

DIRECTIONS Combine each of the following groups of short sentences into one effective sentence. Express the most important idea in the main clause and put lesser ideas in subordinate clauses, phrases, or words. Use coordination only for ideas of equal importance.

1. Young couples in many societies expect help from their parents after they are married. In America newly married couples are expected to survive without help. They must do so to prove themselves independent and mature. They must often suffer great deprivation during the most difficult period of their marriage.

_____

_____

_____

_____

2. The young couple try to be entirely independent of their parents. Their independence usually entails adopting a pattern of living that they consider different from their parents'. They choose instead a pattern that fits the style of the class or clique which they have chosen for themselves.

_____

_____

_____

_____

3. The husband in many societies is the patriarchal breadwinner. He rules his own home. The American marriage ideal requires that the couple plan everything together. The wife is recognized as an equal partner in making decisions.

_____

_____

4. In other societies respect for the past is a basic quality of a marriage. In America the past must be repudiated. The couple must live for the present and for the future. They must live for the better job, the better home, the better way of life.

_____

_____

_____

_____

5. The couple must discount any past loves. They must live only for the present relationship. This relationship will last forever they assume. At least it will if their love is "the real thing."

_____

_____

_____

_____

NAME _____ SCORE _____

DIRECTIONS   Rewrite each of the following stringy sentences to make one effective sentence. Express the most important idea in the main clause and put lesser ideas in subordinate clauses, phrases, or words. Use coordination only for ideas of equal importance.

EXAMPLE

In America there are no requirements for marriage, and so all the couple have to do is to obtain a license, and the license permits them to have the marriage ceremony performed.

Since there are no requirements for marriage in America, all the couple have to do is to obtain a license which permits them to have the marriage ceremony performed.

1. Divorce is fairly commonplace in America, and it gives the couple the freedom to leave each other and establish a new relationship, and the new marriage will then become "the real thing."

   _____

   _____

   _____

   _____

2. Divorce places two new burdens on the couple, and one is a sense of failure in a relationship that is supposed to be permanent, and the other is a feeling of insecurity about everything in life.

   _____

   _____

   _____

   _____

3. A man is always in danger of losing his job and his home, but once he could count on keeping his wife, but today his marriage is no longer a source of security, and so he has nothing he can feel confident of not losing.

---

4. Both husband and wife feel the pressure of the possibility of a divorce, and both must constantly work to see that they are rechosen each day by their mates, and so their marriage becomes something they must always concentrate on.

---

5. Americans value their right to be free to choose, and choices include marriage partners as well as homes and jobs, so Margaret Mead does not feel that we are likely to outlaw divorce, but she does think that we must develop customs to fit the fragile conditions of marriage today.

25

Avoid needless separation of related parts of the sentence. Avoid dangling modifiers.

Every sentence should be so constructed that the relationships among its several parts will be clear to the reader at a glance. Modifiers should be placed as close as possible to the words they modify.

25a   Avoid needless separation of related parts of the sentence.

(1) In standard written English, adverbs such as *almost*, *only*, *just*, *even*, *hardly*, *nearly*, or *merely* are regularly placed immediately before the words they modify.

In spoken English, which tends to place these adverbs before the verb, ambiguity can be prevented by stressing the word to be modified. In written English, however, clarity is ensured only by correct placement of adverbs.

> INFORMAL   The folk singer *only* sang one song.
> GENERAL   The folk singer sang *only one song.*

(2) The position of a modifying prepositional phrase should clearly indicate what the phrase modifies.

A prepositional phrase used as an adjective nearly always immediately follows the word modified.

> MISPLACED   I gave my dress to Mary *with the low neckline.*
> CLEAR   I gave my *dress with the low neckline* to Mary.

(3) Adjective clauses should be placed near the words they modify.

> AWKWARD   He bought the vest at a men's clothing store *which cost only five dollars.* [*Which* does not refer to *store.*]
> CLEAR   At a men's clothing store, he bought the *vest, which cost only five dollars.* [*Which* refers to *vest.*]

(4) Avoid "squinting" constructions—modifiers that may refer either to a preceding or to a following word.

> SQUINTING   I decided *on the next day* to take a vacation.
> CLEAR   I decided *to take a vacation on the next day.*   OR   *On the next day I decided* to take a vacation.

(5) Avoid awkward separation of parts of verb phrases and awkward splitting of infinitives.

AWKWARD	There sat my grandmother, whom we *had* early that morning *put* on the plane.
IMPROVED	There sat my grandmother, whom we *had put* on the plane early that morning.
AWKWARD	She had decided *to,* in a moment of fear, *get off* the plane.
IMPROVED	In a moment of fear she had decided *to get off* the plane. [In general avoid the "split" infinitive unless it is needed for smoothness or clarity.]

Note: Although all split infinitives were once considered questionable, those which are not awkward are now acceptable.

25b Avoid dangling modifiers.

A participle, a gerund, an infinitive, or an elliptical clause or phrase should have in the same sentence a word to which it is clearly and logically related. Otherwise, it is said to "dangle." Eliminate such errors (1) by recasting the sentence to make the dangling element agree with the subject of the main clause or (2) by expanding the phrase or elliptical clause into a subordinate clause. (Do not mistake a transitional expression like *to sum up* for a dangling modifier: see **12b**.)

(1) Dangling participial phrase

DANGLING	*Shouldering our knapsacks,* the hike began. [*Shouldering* does not refer to *knapsacks,* nor to any other word in the sentence.]
IMPROVED	*Shouldering* (OR *Having shouldered*) *our knapsacks, we* began the hike. [*Shouldering* refers to *we,* the subject of the sentence.]
EXPANDED	*After we had shouldered our knapsacks,* the hike began. [Participial phrase expanded into a clause]

(2) Dangling gerund phrase

DANGLING	*On arriving at the river,* the current was frightening.
IMPROVED	*On arriving at the river, we* were frightened by the current.
EXPANDED	*When we arrived at the river,* the current was frightening.

(3) Dangling infinitive phrase

DANGLING	*To hike well,* endurance is needed.
IMPROVED	*To hike well, one* needs endurance.
EXPANDED	*If one is to hike well,* endurance is needed.

(4) Dangling elliptical clause (or phrase)

An elliptical clause—that is, a clause with an implied subject and verb—"dangles" unless the implied subject is the same as that of the main clause.

DANGLING	*When only a baby* (OR *At the age of six months*), her father taught her to swim. [*She was* is implied in the elliptical clause.]
IMPROVED	*When only a baby* (OR *At the age of six months*), *she* was taught to swim by her father.
EXPANDED	*When she was only a baby* (OR *When she was six months old*), her father taught her to swim.

Misplaced parts

NAME _____ SCORE _____

DIRECTIONS   Some of the sentences below are incoherent because of misplaced
parts. First, circle the misplaced word, phrase, or clause; then draw an arrow indi-
cating the correct placement. In the blank at the right, enter (1) the word or (2) the
first and last words of the phrase or clause. (Change capitalization and add punctuation if necessary.) If the sentence is correct, write *C* in the blank at the right.

EXAMPLE

Divorce statistics have (in this country) appalled most
people.   *in — country*

1. In past times a couple were expected to for all
   their lives remain married regardless of the success of their relationship.   _____

2. Of course some couples found their own ways to
   cope with unhappy marital situations who wanted
   to be free.   _____

3. Henry VIII, for example, only lived a short while
   with the wives he grew tired of.   _____

4. Henry was notorious for sending wives to the
   block or to confinement who displeased him.   _____

5. Henry was the king who to be rid of his first wife
   instituted divorce.   _____

6. There were ways to escape the confinement of
   marriage practiced by Europeans for centuries
   other than those of Henry VIII.   _____

7. A man did not just have to settle for one woman
   in his life simply because he married only one.   _____

8. He could marry one woman without being publicly censored and maintain another as his mistress.   _____

9. The man had to have certain things to maintain a
   successful relationship with both his wife and his
   mistress such as money and discretion.   _____

10. Wives, too, were permitted to in some instances
    maintain lovers.   _____

11. A wife could in her home maintain a lover if her husband approved. _____

12. A husband might give such approval to a wife who was many years younger than he. _____

13. Some men thus lived quite openly in a household like Lord Byron. _____

14. Byron, as it happened, was asked to eventually leave the household. _____

15. But, interestingly enough, the reason was a political disagreement with the lady's husband for Byron's dismissal. _____

16. Studies seem to in our time suggest that the mistress or lover is not an outdated convention. _____

17. Today couples have found many ways to pursue other love interests while they are married. _____

18. Wife swapping is in some areas of the country reportedly very popular. _____

19. Orgies were not confined only to Roman times which are today referred to as group sex. _____

20. Studies show, however, that infidelity is not as rampant as articles in magazines and newspapers would lead one to think among married couples. _____

NAME _____ SCORE _____

DIRECTIONS A dangling modifier fails to refer clearly and logically to some word in the sentence. In the following sentences correct any dangling modifier by (1) recasting or rearranging the sentence to make the dangling element agree with the subject of the main clause or by (2) expanding the phrase or elliptical clause into a subordinate clause. Be sure, in the course of correcting the sentences, that you use *both* methods of correction. Show how you have made the correction by writing *subject* or *sub. clause* in the blank at the right. If the sentence is correct, write *C* in the blank at the right.

EXAMPLES

the divorce rate in is
Having tripled since the 1920's, America ~~has an~~ appalling.   *subject*

divorce rate. When one considers
~~Considering~~ the divorce rate, the average American's dis-illusionment with marriage is not surprising.   *sub. clause*

1. When not nearly as serious a problem as now, a Denver judge decided that something had to be done about America's escalating divorce rate. _____

2. Taking a close look at the difficulties besetting American marriages, a plan to allow trial marriages was his suggestion. _____

3. If proved unsatisfactory, a childless couple could dissolve their marriage by mutual consent. _____

4. Denounced for his views, the press and the pulpit gave the judge no rest. _____

5. Finally the judge was dismissed from the bench, after being labeled a heathen and a defiler of the American home. _____

6. No longer regarded as a bizarre possibility, many Americans accept the concept of trial marriage. _____

7. To cope with new attitudes toward morality, a less structured marriage arrangement than what we practice today is recommended by Margaret Mead. _____

8. Issued a kind of preliminary contract, a couple would begin a marriage that could easily be dissolved if their relationship proved unsatisfactory. _____

9. After proving themselves capable of a successful relationship, a final marriage contract would be issued to the couple. _____

10. The final contract having been agreed upon, the couple would then be free to plan a family. _____

11. To protect the children, divorce among married couples with families should be difficult according to Margaret Mead. _____

12. If childless, however, divorce should be a fairly simple procedure for the couple with no shame or guilt attached. _____

13. To sum up, divorce should be easy for those who do not wish to have children but difficult for those who have children. _____

14. Disagreeing with Margaret Mead, trial marriage is still seen by many people as promoting infidelity and impermanent relationships. _____

15. To counter the rising divorce rate, our belief in the sanctity of marriage should be restored. _____

16. Convinced of the value of fidelity and permanence, marriages would not fail as frequently as they do today. _____

26

Parallel ideas should be expressed in parallel structure.

26a Coordinate ideas are clearer to the reader when they are expressed in parallel structure.

To express coordinate ideas a noun should be balanced with a noun, an active verb with an active verb, an infinitive with an infinitive, a subordinate clause with a subordinate clause, a main clause with a main clause.

AWKWARD Let us remember *his love* and *that he was kind*. [Noun paralleled with a subordinate clause]

PARALLEL *Let us remember* ‖ *his love* and
‖ *his kindness.*

OR

Let us remember ‖ *that he loved us* and
‖ *that he was kind.*

AWKWARD *To sleep* and *eating* were his main occupations. [Infinitive paralleled with a gerund]

PARALLEL ‖ *To sleep* and
‖ *to eat*
were his main occupations.

OR

‖ *Eating* and
‖ *sleeping*
were his main occupations.

26b Repetition of a preposition, an article, an auxiliary verb, the sign of the infinitive, or the introductory word of a long phrase or clause is often necessary to make the parallel clear.

AWKWARD I envy the mayor *for his privileges*, but not *his responsibilities*.

IMPROVED I envy the mayor ‖ *for his privileges*, but not
‖ *for his responsibilities.*

AWKWARD At the party I talked to *a doctor* and *lawyer*.

IMPROVED At the party I talked to ‖ *a doctor* and
‖ *a lawyer.*

26c Correlatives (*either . . . or, neither . . . nor, both . . . and, not only . . . but also, whether . . . or*) should be followed by elements that are parallel in form.

FAULTY She was *not only pretty but also knew how to dress well*. [Adjective paralleled with a verb]

BETTER She was ‖ *not only pretty*
BETTER ‖ *but also well dressed.*

27

Avoid needless shifts in point of view.

27a   Needless shift in tense

SHIFT   The boy *ate* the candy and *throws* the wrapper on the floor.   [Shift from past tense to present tense]

BETTER   The boy *ate* the candy and *threw* the wrapper on the floor.   [Both verbs in the past tense]

27b   Needless shift in mood

SHIFT   First *listen* intently and then you *should take* notes.   [Shift from imperative to indicative mood]

BETTER   First *listen* intently and then *take* notes.   [Both verbs in the imperative mood]

27c   Needless shift in subject or voice

A shift in subject often involves a shift in voice. A shift in voice nearly always involves a shift in subject.

SHIFT   Ann liked tennis, but ping-pong was also enjoyed by her.   [The subject shifts from *Ann* to *ping-pong*. The voice shifts from active to passive.]

BETTER   Ann liked tennis, but she also enjoyed ping-pong.   [One subject only. Both verbs are active.]

27d   Needless shift in person

SHIFT   If *a person* reads well, *you* will probably succeed in school.   [Shift from third person to second person]

BETTER   If *a person* reads well, *he* will probably succeed in school.

27e   Needless shift in number

SHIFT   *One* should vote to express *their* political views.   [Shift from singular *one* to plural *their*]

BETTER   *One* should vote to express *his* (OR *one's*) political views.

27f   Needless shift from indirect to direct discourse

SHIFT   Sue asked *whether I knew* the nominee and *will he be* a good sheriff.   [Mixed indirect and direct discourse]

BETTER   Sue asked *whether I knew* the nominee and *whether he would be* a good sheriff.   [Indirect discourse]   OR
Sue asked, "*Do you know* the nominee? *Will he be* a good sheriff?"   [Direct discourse]

Parallelism

NAME _____ SCORE _____

DIRECTIONS   In each of the following sentences underscore the parts having parallel ideas that should be expressed in parallel structure. Revise each sentence to make the parts parallel and enter the key word or words of the revision in the blank at the right.

EXAMPLE

Recently there have been many plans suggested
to curb
~~for curbing~~ the rising divorce rate and to
insure^ happy marriages.   *to curb*

1. One plan has been suggested by Norman Sheresky and Marya Mannes and appearing in a book entitled *Uncoupling: The Art of Coming Apart.*   _____

2. Sheresky and Mannes argue that marriage should be difficult to get into rather than making it hard to get out of.   _____

3. They think that couples should be made to consider not only the advantages of matrimony but also what the obligations are.   _____

4. In advance of matrimony a couple should spend the time required for talking over and to write out their expectations for marriage.   _____

5. They should list their intentions with regard to place of residence, to children, and religion.   _____

6. In the contract the couple should furnish each other an account of their backgrounds, including such items as parental upbringing, educational achievement, and what their general salary levels have been.   _____

7. They should outline what their relationships with their families have been as well as their expectations for their future relationships.

_____

8. For example, if the wife-to-be typically visits her parents once a week, then the contract should specify whether the husband-to-be finds this arrangement acceptable and will he agree to go with her on such visits.

_____

9. The contract should itemize the types of behavior that the couple will not tolerate in addition to their preferences in behavior.

_____

10. The contract should spell out in full and exactly the couple's attitudes toward sex.

_____

11. The couple should agree in advance of matrimony to a plan for a property settlement and how to support their children should their marriage end in separation or divorce.

_____

12. To many couples such a contract would seem difficult and demand a great deal.

_____

13. One could argue that many couples would find the contract too much trouble and they would decide against marriage.

_____

14. Sheresky and Mannes claim that the purpose of the contract is to make such couples think hard about matrimony and the prevention of those couples from marrying who are not willing to face up to the realities of marriage.

_____

15. Marriage, Sheresky and Mannes believe, is viewed too lightly and without enough realism.

_____

Shifts in point of view

NAME _____ SCORE _____

DIRECTIONS   Indicate the kind of shift in each of the following sentences by mark-
ing in the blank at the right *a* (tense), *b* (mood), *c* (subject-voice), *d* (person), *e*
(number), or *f* (discourse). Make the necessary corrections.

EXAMPLE

Each person has ~~their~~ *his* own opinion about what is right and wrong
with modern marriages.   *e*

1. When one studies modern marriages, you realize that couples
   today face many problems that once did not exist.   _____

2. Prior to World War II few married women worked outside
   the home, and if a woman did work, their career was usually
   secondary to their homemaking.   _____

3. Today more than half the married women in America work
   outside the home, and their careers are valued by many as
   much as their homemaking.   _____

4. If a woman is trained in college to pursue a given career,
   they do not like to forget about it simply because they get
   married.   _____

5. Look around and you should notice that many women are
   pursuing careers as aggressively as men are.   _____

6. Many men have been conditioned to think that a woman's
   place is in the home and were not able to accept the new
   career-minded woman.   _____

7. At the same time, many a married woman who pursues a
   career feels that they are somehow doing the wrong thing.   _____

8. The working mother often does not know whether she should
   think first of her obligation to her family or should she give
   first consideration to her career.   _____

9. More than one woman who works finds themselves burdened
   with all the housework and child care when they arrive home
   in the evening.   _____

10. From the magazine and newspaper articles we read, you realize that many couples are solving the problem of the working wife and mother in a way that satisfies them. _____

11. When both husband and wife work, they often arranged the household duties so that each did his share. _____

12. An even more innovative plan used by some couples today calls for the wife to stay home one year or more while the husband worked and then for the wife to pursue her career while the husband minded the home. _____

13. In some instances couples have found that their careers demand they were in different areas of the state or country. _____

14. Many of these couples have worked out an arrangement whereby they spend their weekdays apart pursuing their different careers and their weekends together when each person can devote themselves exclusively to their marriage. _____

15. Whatever one thinks about the various arrangements modern couples have devised, you must agree that most women who have careers they enjoy are not going to give them up. _____

16. Thus we must find patterns of living that accommodate the changes that had occurred within the family during the last few decades. _____

28

Make every pronoun refer unmistakably and definitely to its antecedent.

A pronoun has meaning only if the reader understands the antecedent (usually a noun or another pronoun) to which it refers. If the reader cannot determine the antecedent at first glance, the sentence should be recast.

28a   Avoid ambiguous reference.

Do not cause the reader to hesitate between two antecedents.

AMBIGUOUS   Mary told Laura that she had used her perfume.   [Who had used whose perfume?]

CLEAR   Mary said to Laura, "I have used your perfume." OR Mary said to Laura, "You have used my perfume."

28b   Avoid remote reference.

Do not refer to an antecedent too far removed from the pronoun. Usually a clear antecedent will come within the same sentence as the pronoun or in the sentence immediately preceding.

REMOTE   The lake covers many acres. Near the shore, water lilies grow in profusion, spreading out their green leaves and sending up white blossoms on slender stems. *It* is well stocked with fish.   [The pronoun *it* is too far removed from its antecedent *lake*.]

IMPROVED   . . . The *lake* is well stocked with fish.   [Repetition of the antecedent *lake*]

VAGUE   Jon went to the beach to look for a starfish to add to his collection. *It* was usually covered with shells.   [Temporarily confusing: the antecedent of *it* is not clear until the reader finishes the sentence.]

CLEAR   Jon went to the *beach, which* was usually covered with shells, to look for a starfish to add to his collection.   [The pronoun *which* is placed next to its antecedent, *beach*.]

OBSCURE   When Bob's health studio was begun, *he* asked me to be a customer.   [Reference to antecedent in the possessive case]

IMPROVED   When *Bob* began his health studio, *he* asked me to be a customer.

28c   Use broad reference only with discretion.

As a rule avoid *broad* reference (1) to the general idea of a preceding clause or sentence, (2) to a noun not expressed but merely inferred from a verb or some other word, or (3) to some indefinite antecedent by the use of *they, you,* or *it*.[1] That is, ordinarily use a pronoun only when it has as its antecedent some specific noun or word used as a noun.

VAGUE   Many college students travel to Europe for the summer. This gives them the opportunity to learn a second language and to experience a different culture from the one they have grown up in. [*This* has no antecedent.]

CLEAR   The many college students who travel to Europe for the summer have an opportunity to learn a second language and to experience a different culture from the one they have grown up in. [The vague pronoun is eliminated.]

VAGUE   In one of Wordsworth's poems it tells about a young man who is corrupted by city life.

CLEAR   One of Wordsworth's poems tells about a young man who is corrupted by city life.

COLLOQUIAL   At college they expect students to take care of themselves.

CLEAR   At college students are expected to take care of themselves.

28d   Avoid the confusion arising from the repetition in the same sentence of a pronoun referring to different antecedents.

CONFUSING   Although it is very hot by the lake, it looks inviting. [The first *it* is an expletive; the second *it* refers to *lake*.]

CLEAR   Although it is very hot by the lake, the water looks inviting.

CONFUSING   We should have prepared for our examinations earlier. It is too late to do it now.

CLEAR   We should have prepared for our examinations earlier. It is too late to prepare now.

[1] Informal English allows much latitude in the use of antecedents that must be inferred from the context. Even standard or formal English sometimes accepts the general idea of a clause as an antecedent when the reference is unmistakable. But it is generally wise for the inexperienced writer to make each of his pronouns refer to a specific noun or pronoun.

NAME _____ SCORE _____

DIRECTIONS   In the following sentences mark a capital *V* through each pronoun that makes a vague reference and enter the pronoun in the blank at the right. Recast the sentence or sentences to clarify the meaning.

EXAMPLE

Not all people are interested in preserving marriage. They believe this is an outdated institution.   *this*

1. Some people believe it is time we recognize that marriage is no longer compatible with today's life style. They believe it is now necessary to replace it with a new type of relationship.   _____

2. These people believe that modern couples need to be free to change partners whenever they choose, which is the reason for the current high divorce rate.   _____

3. They do not believe that couples should have to bind themselves to lifetime commitments and to the infringements of freedom that accompany them.   _____

4. Because of the marriage contract neither the man nor the woman feels free to do what he wants when he wants, and this makes each feel trapped.   _____

5. In the book *Open Marriage* it recommends that couples grant each other more freedom of movement within the framework of marriage.   _____

6. But those who rebel against the institution of marriage see no reason for a couple's having to grant each other this since it should be a basic right of each individual.   _____

7. In Byron's *Don Juan* he sets forth much the same arguments against marriage that the modern spokesman does.   _____

8. When Juan said to Lambro that he truly loved his daughter, he had made all the moral commitment that Byron felt was necessary. _____

9. Haidée, Lambro's daughter, did not ask for any vows of constancy, and it made Juan very happy with her. _____

10. Today many couples live together for many years without ever marrying, which does not shock the general public as much as it once did. _____

11. Twenty years ago Ingrid Bergman left her husband for another man and was branded an immoral woman for it. _____

12. Today one reads about many Hollywood couples who openly live together without being married, and it does not seem to shock many people. _____

13. They say that people have a right to do whatever pleases them as long as they do not hurt others. _____

14. Those who speak out against marriage do not feel that couples who live together without being married are hurting anyone by this. _____

15. Sometimes when an unmarried couple have a child, it forces them to consider marriage. _____

16. But many couples have children and never marry. Birth certificates no longer list illegitimate births. Thus they do not feel the pressure to marry that they once would have felt to prevent their children from being publicly ridiculed. _____

29

Select words and arrange the parts of the sentence to give emphasis to important ideas.

Some ideas deserve more stress than others. A writer can emphasize these ideas by varying the normal sentence word order. A factual reporting of snows in March might read: "The snows came in March." But if snows were unusual in March or if they affected the writer in an unusual way, he might write: "In March came the snows." By varying from subject-verb word order, the writer has called attention to the importance of the snows.

Obviously, emphatic sentence patterns must be saved for ideas that deserve special stress; if used too often the writer's style will appear stilted. A sports article that reads "Down the field ran the quarterback. Across the goal went he. The crowd cheered; the team chanted. Won was the game" calls undue attention to every idea. The reader will doubtless be more amused than impressed with the article.

Emphatic word order, used at the proper time, is a quality of good style.

29a   Gain emphasis by placing important words at the beginning or end of the sentence—especially at the end.

WEAK   The Senate will now pass the bill, in all probability.   [The weakest part of the sentence is given the most emphatic position—the end.]

EMPHATIC   In all probability, the Senate will now pass the bill.   [Strong end] OR   The Senate, in all probability, will now pass the bill.   [Most emphatic—strong beginning and end]

29b   Gain emphasis by changing loose sentences into periodic sentences.

A sentence that holds the reader in suspense until the end is called *periodic;* one that makes a complete statement and then adds details is called *loose.* Both types of sentences are good. The more common loose sentence makes for easy reading. But the periodic sentence, by reserving the main idea until the end, is more emphatic. Note the difference in tone in the following sentences.

LOOSE   Remember names if you want to run for public office.   [Clear sentence]

PERIODIC   If you want to run for public office, remember names.   [More emphatic]

Note that this technique is an extension of the principle presented in **29a.**

29c   Gain emphasis by arranging ideas in the order of climax.

UNEMPHATIC   He pledged her his love, his time, and his money.

EMPHATIC   He pledged her his money, his time, and his love.

29d   Gain emphasis by using the active instead of the passive voice.

WEAK   Daily calls to his fiancée were made by him.
STRONG   He made daily calls to his fiancée.

29e   Gain emphasis by repeating important words.

EMPHATIC   We longed for the days of our youth, for the days of new love, for the days of great dreams and desires.

29f   Gain emphasis by putting a word or phrase out of its usual order.

UNEMPHATIC   The war was finally ended.
EMPHATIC   Finally ended was the war.

This technique for gaining emphasis should be used sparingly to avoid making the writer's style artificial.

29g   Gain emphasis by using balanced sentences.

UNBALANCED   It is human to err, but to forgive is divine.
BALANCED   To err is human, to forgive divine.

NAME _____ SCORE _____

DIRECTIONS   Enter *a, b, c, d, e, f,* or *g* in the blank at the right to indicate that each
of the following sentences is unemphatic chiefly because of (a) the ineffective placement of important words, (b) the use of loose instead of periodic structure, (c) the
lack of climactic order, (d) the use of the passive instead of the active voice, (e) the
failure to repeat important words, (f) the failure to move a word or phrase from its
usual order, or (g) the lack of proper balance. Revise the sentences to make them
emphatic.

EXAMPLE

To be sure,
~~t~~ The battle between the sexes is an old one~~y. to be sure.~~   *a*

1. Even the first man and woman quarreled, according to the
   Bible.   _____

2. After the forbidden fruit was eaten, harsh words were ex-
   changed by Adam and Eve.   _____

3. Adam accused Eve of causing their downfall; their downfall
   was blamed on Adam by Eve.   _____

4. Adam and Eve were eventually reconciled to each other,
   nevertheless.   _____

5. They knew that they could not live without each other, that
   they loved each other, and that they wanted each other.   _____

6. We learn that men and women have been quarreling and
   then reconciling ever since Adam and Eve's time when we
   study history, literature, and sociology.   _____

7. Male and female relationships are as complex as men and
   women themselves are, not surprisingly.   _____

8. The differences between male and female psychologies often
   separate the two sexes; the attraction of the two sexes is just
   as often based on these differences.   _____

9. There are many theories about the direction male-female
   relationships are taking during the 1970's, of course.   _____

10. Some theories are optimistic about the future of male-female relationships; pessimism characterizes other theories. _____

11. The battle between the sexes has been long and hard fought. _____

12. The battle between the sexes is a conflict of words, gestures, even facial expressions. _____

13. The battle is fought in the homes of the rich; the houses of the poor experience it. _____

14. The winner of the conflict will never be decided, in all probability. _____

15. The battle between the sexes may well be the most significant battle when all of mankind's wars have been evaluated. _____

30

Vary the structure and length of your sentences to make your whole composition pleasing and effective.

A monotonous repetition of the same sentence structure and the same sentence length throughout a paragraph will tire the reader. The effective writer changes the pace of his composition by varying the length and the structure of his sentences, and by varying the beginnings, as this short paragraph from Jacques Barzun's "In Favor of Capital Punishment" illustrates:

> But why kill? I am ready to believe the statistics tending to show that the prospect of his own death does not stop the murderer. For one thing he is often a blind egotist, who cannot conceive the possibility of his own death. For another, detection would have to be infallible to deter the more imaginative who, although afraid, think they can escape discovery. Lastly, as Shaw long ago pointed out, hanging the wrong man will deter as effectively as hanging the right one. So, once again, why kill? If I agree that moral progress means an increasing respect for human life, how can I oppose abolition?[1]

30a   Avoid the monotonous style that usually results from a series of short simple sentences.

MONOTONOUS

[1]Sometimes one consults an expert about a problem. [2]The expert behaves in a strange way. [3]He pretends not to know what is wrong. [4]He asks the amateur to diagnose the problem. [5]He asks him, "What do you think is wrong with your car or radio or physical condition?" [6]This approach seems strange. [7]The expert is supposed to be the one who can determine what is wrong with the car or radio or human body. [8]Yet sometimes the expert's knowledge gets in his way. [9]He knows too much to diagnose a simple problem. [10]He knows too many things that may be at fault. [11]The amateur knows very few facts about the car or radio or human body. [12]But he may immediately identify the problem.

VARIED

[1]Sometimes when one consults an expert about a problem, the expert behaves strangely. [2]Pretending not to know what is wrong, he asks the amateur to diagnose the problem. [3]He asks him, "What do you think is wrong with your car or radio or physical condition?" [4]This approach seems strange because the expert is supposed to be the one who can determine what is wrong with the car or radio or human body. [5]Yet sometimes because of his wide knowledge, the expert may be unable to diagnose a simple problem. [6]He knows too many things that may be at fault. [7]The amateur, who knows very few facts about the car or radio or human body, may immediately identify the problem.

---

[1] "In Favor of Capital Punishment," *American Scholar*, 31, 2 (Spring 1962), 183.

Notice that most of the short sentences in the first paragraph have been rewritten as longer sentences in the second paragraph. Sentence 6 in the second paragraph is then shorter than the surrounding sentences; consequently, it receives emphasis that it did not have in the first paragraph.

30b   Avoid a long series of sentences beginning with the subject by varying the beginnings of sentences.

(1) Begin with an adverb or an adverb phrase or clause.

ADVERB   The quarterback listened to the coach's instructions. *Then* the team discussed the upcoming play in the huddle.

ADVERB PHRASE   *After listening to the coach's instructions,* the quarterback discussed the upcoming play in the huddle.

ADVERB CLAUSE   *After the quarterback had listened to the coach's instructions,* he discussed the upcoming play in the huddle.

(2) Begin with a prepositional phrase or a participial phrase.

PREPOSITIONAL PHRASE   *In the huddle* the team discussed the upcoming play.

PARTICIPIAL PHRASE   *Huddling at mid-field,* the team discussed the upcoming play.

(3) Begin with a coordinating conjunction such as *and, but, or, nor,* or *yet* when the conjunction can be used to show the proper relation of the sentence to the preceding sentence.

When the quarterback returned to the huddle with the coach's instructions, the team discussed the upcoming play with enthusiasm. *And* they came up to the line ready to make the double reverse gain them a touchdown.

30c   Avoid the loose, stringy compound sentence. (See also **24b**.)

The use of loose, stringy compound sentences results in a style that is as monotonous as that created by a series of short simple sentences.

LOOSE AND STRINGY   Sometimes one consults an expert about a problem, and the expert behaves in a strange way.

EFFECTIVE   Sometimes when one consults an expert about a problem, the expert behaves in a strange way.   [Complex sentence]

LOOSE AND STRINGY   He pretends not to know what is wrong, and he asks the amateur to diagnose the problem.

EFFECTIVE   Pretending not to know what is wrong, he asks the amateur to diagnose the problem.   [Participial phrase and main clause]

NAME _____ SCORE _____

DIRECTIONS   Write sentences to illustrate the various types specified below.

1. a simple sentence (**1e**)

2. a compound sentence (**1e**)

3. a simple sentence with a compound predicate (**12a**)

4. a complex sentence (**1e**)

5. a compound-complex sentence (**1e**)

6. a sentence beginning with an adverb phrase (**30b**)

7. the same sentence beginning with a prepositional phrase (**30b**)

8. the same sentence beginning with an adverb clause (**30b**)

9. the same sentence beginning with a participial phrase (**30b**)

10. the same sentence beginning with a coordinating conjunction (**30b**)

11. a loose sentence (**29b**)

12. a balanced sentence (**29g**)

13. a periodic sentence (**29b**)

NAME _____ SCORE _____

DIRECTIONS   Analyze the use of varied sentence lengths and structures in the paragraph by Jacques Barzun on page 145 by answering the following questions:

1. How many short sentences does Barzun use?

2. Where are they located in the paragraph?

3. How many loose, stringy compound sentences does Barzun use?

4. How many sentences does he begin with something other than the subject?

5. Name the structures that he uses to vary from subject-first word order.

6. Does Barzun use any kind of sentence other than the declarative sentence?

NAME _____ SCORE _____

DIRECTIONS Analyze the causes for the monotonous style of the following paragraph by answering the questions printed below it. Then revise the paragraph to introduce sentences that vary in both length and structure.

PARAGRAPH

¹Extreme dependency is often overlooked as a cause for marital discord, and it accounts for perhaps 50 percent of the anger and resentment husbands and wives may feel for each other. ²The wife is the one who is most often dependent on her husband. ³She thinks marriage entails extreme dependency. ⁴She cannot make a decision without her husband's guidance. ⁵She consults him about the simplest of household decisions. ⁶She asks him, for example, at which supermarket she should shop. ⁷She asks what laundry detergent she should use. ⁸She feels inadequate to assume any responsibility in the marriage. ⁹She says with a smile, "I couldn't find my way home from town without my husband's help." ¹⁰The husband perhaps laughs and calls her his little scatterbrained wife, and he may seem outwardly pleased with her dependency. ¹¹He may be seething inside at her inability to act on her own, and he may feel disgust for her demands on his time and energy.

1. How many of the sentences in the paragraph begin with something other than the subject?   _____

2. Which sentences are loose, stringy compound sentences?   _____

3. Which sentences are a series of short sentences?   _____

REVISION

EFFECTIVE COMPOSITIONS

The Paragraph   ¶ 31

31

Develop ideas adequately into unified and coherent paragraphs.

A paragraph is a distinct unit of thought that develops one central idea fully. Each sentence in the paragraph is carefully related to the other sentences and thus moves the development of the paragraph along toward a unified and coherent treatment of the central idea. The ordinary paragraphs that one sees in current books and magazines vary in length from about 50 to 250 words, with the average length being about 100 words. The first line of a paragraph is indented to signal the beginning of the development of a new central idea.

31a Make each sentence in the paragraph contribute to the central idea or thought.

The central idea or thought (often called the topic sentence) is the controlling sentence in the paragraph; it determines the content of all other sentences in the paragraph. Because it is the controlling sentence, the central idea usually appears as the first or second sentence in the paragraph, but it may appear elsewhere in the paragraph, even at the end if the paragraph is intended to have a kind of dramatic build up. Wherever the central idea is placed, the writer must be conscious of it in planning all his other sentences if the paragraph is to have unity.

The central idea or thought is printed in italics in the paragraph below. Notice how each of the other sentences in the paragraph is carefully related to this controlling idea.

[1]Sport may be the last great stronghold against female equality. [2]*In no other field is there so little female representation as in organized sport.* [3]There are virtually no female athletes other than gymnasts, swimmers, ice skaters, tennis players, and runners. [4]And even these female athletes are encouraged to complete their participation early in life so that they can devote themselves to being women. [5]One rarely hears about a female of mature years playing football, basketball, or baseball—the traditional American sports that are supposed to develop the qualities needed for leadership in our country. [6]One looks hard, too, for a female referee or umpire, a female sportscaster or sports reporter, a female coach. [7]In short, women exist on the sidelines of the great American games: women are the short-skirted cheerleaders and the scantily clad baton twirlers and pompom girls.

The unity of the preceding paragraph can be destroyed by inserting any sentence that is not a part of the plan called for by the central idea. Try reading the paragraph with this sentence inserted between sentences 4 and 5:

To be truly feminine, women should spend their time at beauty shops, P.T.A. meetings, and bridge parties to satisfy their interests outside the home. This one sentence, if not enclosed in parentheses, would shift the direction of the paragraph away from women in organized sport—the direction called for by the central idea. To maintain unity in a paragraph, then, the writer must be conscious of his central idea each time he adds a sentence.

31b Interlink the sentences in the paragraph so that the thought flows smoothly from one sentence to the next.

A coherent paragraph is one in which the relationship of any given sentence to the one before or after it is clear and the transitions between the sentences are smooth. A coherent paragraph is easy to read because the sentences flow along with no jarring breaks; the sentences are arranged in a clear, logical order, and one or more methods of achieving smooth transitions between sentences has been used—pronouns with antecedents in preceding sentences, repeated words or ideas, transitional expressions, and parallel structure.

(1) Arrange the sentences in a clear, logical order.

There are three commonly used plans for arranging sentences in a logical order: time or chronological order for narrative paragraphs, space order (near to far, far to near, left to right) for descriptive paragraphs, order of climax (least important to most important or least familiar to most familiar or vice versa) for explanatory or persuasive paragraphs.

(2) Link sentences by using pronouns referring to antecedents in the preceding sentences. (See also Section **28**.)

(3) Link sentences by repeating key words or ideas from the preceding sentences.

(4) Link sentences by using such transitional expressions as *however, but, therefore, furthermore, then, and,* and *to sum up.*

(5) Link sentences by using parallel structure—that is, by repeating a sentence pattern.

The following paragraph illustrates all five of these ways for achieving coherence in a paragraph. The sentences are arranged in order of climax (least important to most important); methods for achieving smooth transitions between sentences are identified by numbers—2 through 5—that correspond with the numbers in the list just cited.

> There is much evidence that the roles of the sexes are changing. (4) First, and most noticeable, is the change in dress and appearance. In clothing many boys and girls look alike. (2) Their hair may be equally long. (2, 5) Their shirts and pants may be the same. (2, 5) Even their way of moving when walking may be indistinguishable. (4, 3) But equally important evidence of the

shift in sex roles is apparent in the job market. Whereas a generation ago no more than one out of ten women with children under eighteen was employed, today one out of three is working. (4) And jobs that were once considered appropriate only to men are now being filled by women. (4, 3) Conversely, many men today are training to be nurses, secretaries, and airline stewards—positions once considered unmistakably feminine. (4, 3) Finally, the most significant evidence of the changing roles of men and women is the increasing sexual aggressiveness women are demonstrating. (3) Once the man played the role of the seducer. (4, 3) But today the woman is no longer the reticent partner in a sexual relationship. (4, 3) In fact, one out of four women, instead of one out of four men, complains of lack of sexual activity in her relationship. (3) Women today initiate a sexual experience almost as often as men do. (3, 4) This shift toward sexual aggressiveness of the woman is, for many sociologists, the final and convincing proof that the roles of the sexes have undergone a profound change during the last few decades.

31c Develop ideas adequately so that the paragraph presents enough information about the central idea to satisfy the reader.

While some paragraphs are very short, perhaps no longer than one sentence, the majority are six or more sentences in length. There is no specified length that a paragraph must be, but it must present enough information to satisfy the reader, to make him feel that the central idea has been fully explored.

31d Master various methods of paragraph development.

The central idea of a paragraph may be developed in a variety of ways. Some paragraphs use only one method of development while others use two or more.

(1) Use relevant specific details to develop a central idea.

The central idea "Extreme dependency accounts for perhaps 50 percent of the anger and resentment husbands and wives may feel for each other" led one writer to think of various details that show the wife's dependency on the husband and his reaction to her dependency. The resulting paragraph on page 150 is not an illustration of good style, but it does show how a writer can use relevant specific details to support his central idea.

(2) Use several closely related examples or one striking example to illustrate a central idea.

A paragraph developed by examples almost always holds the reader's attention. Examples are frequently used in opening paragraphs of essays or in paragraphs that have central ideas the reader might question, such as the following paragraph:

> [1]There is no place to live that is free from the threat of water. [2]My own experience supports this claim. [3]For five years I lived on the ocean at five feet above sea level. [4]Each time there was a hurricane at sea I had to board up the house and evacuate to higher ground. [5]Finally exhausted from the years of

facing the danger of flooding, I moved to an inland state. [6]Because my home was five hundred feet above sea level, I felt secure from the threat of water. [7]But I had lived there only two weeks when a creek that was barely in view from my house overflowed and sent water flooding into the downstairs of my home. [8]As I watched the muddy water rise two inches, four inches, and finally six inches all over the lower level of my home, I wondered to what safe spot I could move next. [9]Perhaps California.

(3) Use an extended definition to develop a central idea.

Sometimes a writer wants to explain a term more fully or more subjectively than the definition offered by the dictionary. He may use a paragraph or even an entire essay to define a term like *home*.

> [1]A home is, of course, a kind of dwelling, a shelter from the weather. [2]But it is much more than that. [3]If it were not, an office or a store would be a fine place to live. [4]Edgar A. Guest suggested one of the differences between a home and other buildings in his famous line, "It takes a heap o' livin' in a house t' make it home." [5]A home is a very private place where one does very private things, like writing in a diary, sleeping, writing a poem, singing in the shower, loving, and maybe even dying. [6]It's the one place a person can go to get away from people he does not want to see and things he does not want to do. [7]Of course, even the privacy of the home is being invaded today, but it's still the only place left where a person can sit down and cry without being treated for indigestion or depression.

(4) Use classification to develop a central idea.

When a writer uses classification, he divides his subject into categories. The paragraph on page 151 explains the categories of American sport that women do not participate in.

(5) Use comparison or contrast to develop a central idea.

If a writer uses comparison to develop a central idea, he points out similarities between the things he is discussing; if he uses contrast, he points out the differences. The paragraph on pages 152–53 uses both comparison and contrast to develop the central idea that the roles of the sexes are changing.

(6) Use cause or effect to develop a central idea.

In causal analysis the writer explains the reasons for an effect or effects. Jacques Barzun's paragraph on page 145 explains the reasons why capital punishment does not deter the murderer.

(7) Use a combination of methods to develop a central idea.

Various methods of paragraph development have been listed and illustrated. Frequently the writer uses two or more of these methods in a single paragraph to develop his central idea.

NAME _____ SCORE _____

DIRECTIONS   Underline the central idea of the following paragraph. Then circle the numbers of those sentences that interfere with the unity of the paragraph.

¹The question may well be raised: are men and women happy with the changing roles they are experiencing? ²Some sociologists feel there is much evidence to suggest that they are not. ³A study conducted by the Department of Labor revealed that half the married women who were working full time would have preferred part-time work. ⁴Of course, part-time employment still takes women out of the home. ⁵And surely a change from the routine of full-time housework must be welcomed. ⁶A possible reason for women's unhappiness with their jobs is revealed by their salaries: only 1 percent earn $10,000 a year or more. ⁷Here the women's liberation movement can make a good case for discrimination against women rather than lack of ambition. ⁸Feminists argue that women are almost invariably paid less than men who do the same work. ⁹Some employers would challenge this claim by pointing out that women are usually less dependable than men; men simply are not absent from work as often as women. ¹⁰There are also studies to show that men register some disagreement with the changing roles of the sexes. ¹¹A survey conducted by the *Harvard Business Review* determined that more than half of the business executives consulted felt women were "temperamentally unsuited" for management. ¹²Federal employees apparently agree with the business executives: 75 percent of those surveyed claimed that women are not good supervisors. ¹³The sociologists who believe that men and women are not happy with their so-called new identities find the proof overwhelming.

Unity in paragraphs

NAME _____ SCORE _____

DIRECTIONS   Write a central idea in the space provided that will give unity to the sentences included in the following paragraph about the comic strip *Peanuts*.

1   *Charlie Brown feels insecure with ~~females~~ but he ~~still~~ ~~trying~~ attempts ~~attempting~~ to gain some self confidence.*

²Charlie Brown constantly consults Lucy for encouragement, but he usually feels even more insecure after paying her the nickel consultation fee. ³Lucy's usual reply to anything Charlie says is, "You're a blockhead, Charlie Brown." ⁴He has the same unhappy experience with the little red-haired girl he is always trying to get up the nerve to speak to. ⁵He secretly loves her, but he knows she will have nothing to do with him; therefore he pines away, never asking her to walk home from school with him. ⁶Charlie Brown is even insecure around his female teacher. ⁷Since he is certain she does not like him, any correction she makes of his class work becomes positive proof that he is eternally doomed to suffer his teacher's disapproval—and even worse, the scorn of all females.

DIRECTIONS A paragraph, like any other piece of writing, requires planning if it is to have unity. Make notes for a central idea and the supporting points that you can use in a paragraph about a well-known comic-strip couple. (The last paragraph in the preceding exercise made a point about the quality of Charlie Brown's relationship with the females in his life. Your central idea for this paragraph should also make a point about the quality of the relationship between the husband and wife you choose.) Once you have listed the central idea and the points you want to make about it, look over your list carefully to see whether all your ideas support your controlling thought. If any points need to be deleted or rearranged in order, do so before you write the paragraph. (Of course, you may also make changes in order when you actually write the paragraph.) Then compose your paragraph, using your central idea in the first or second sentence.

CENTRAL IDEA

SUPPORTING POINTS

1.

2.

3.

4.

5.

6.

7.

PARAGRAPH

Coherence in paragraphs

NAME _____ SCORE _____

DIRECTIONS   The following paragraph has unity, but it lacks coherence. Rewrite it, supplying the needed coherence. Consult the list on page 152 for guidance in making your revisions. Some sentences will have to be entirely rewritten to achieve smooth transitions; others will need only the addition of a word or two. And several need no changes at all.

PARAGRAPH

¹Most people believe that children cement a husband and wife's relationship. ²An essay by Nigel Balchin entitled "Children Are a Waste of Time" argues differently. ³A man marries a woman whom he wants to be his mistress, his companion, and his wife. ⁴The relationship is changed when she becomes a mother. ⁵A father is not the same as a husband. ⁶The arrival of the "Sacred Calves" changes everything. ⁷Life is to be lived for the children's sake, not for the parents'. ⁸Each generation wastes its energy and time in developing the talents of the next generation rather than its own. ⁹The husband and wife find themselves reading children's stories and playing children's games rather than pursuing their own adult interests. ¹⁰Watching a child smear food over the tray of his highchair does not improve the quality of the parents' meal. ¹¹Sleep is not better because one gets up in the middle of the night with two crying children. ¹²Discipling children is not the most exciting way to spend a day. ¹³It is no wonder that Nigel Balchin argues that children destroy a husband and wife's relationship.

REVISION

Paragraph practice　　　　　　　　　　　　　　　Exercise 31-5

NAME _____ SCORE _____

DIRECTIONS　Using *specific details* as the method of development, write a paragraph on one of the following subjects. First, plan the paragraph as you did for Exercise 31–3; then compose the sentences for the paragraph. You may use details found in the exercises of this book or details from your own knowledge.

SUBJECTS

1. the liberated woman (or man)
2. the typical wife (or husband)
3. a modern marriage contract

CENTRAL IDEA

SUPPORTING POINTS

1.

2.

3.

4.

5.

6.

7.

PARAGRAPH

DIRECTIONS　Using *several closely related examples or one striking example* as the method of development, write a paragraph on one of the following subjects. First, plan the paragraph; then compose the sentences for the paragraph. You may use examples found in the exercises of this book or examples from your own knowledge.

SUBJECTS

1. famous male-female relationships in history
2. famous male-female relationships in literature
3. male-female relationships among animals that parallel human male-female relationships

CENTRAL IDEA

SUPPORTING POINTS

1.

2.

3.

4.

5.

6.

7.

PARAGRAPH

Paragraph practice

NAME _____ SCORE _____

DIRECTIONS   Using *definition* as the method of development, write a paragraph on one of the following subjects. First, plan the paragraph; then compose the sentences for the paragraph. You may use facts found in the exercises of this book or facts from your own knowledge.

SUBJECTS

1. a definition of the male (or female) stereotype
2. a definition of the woman's liberation movement (or male chauvinism)
3. a definition of romantic love (or the American marriage ideal)

CENTRAL IDEA

SUPPORTING POINTS

1.

2.

3.

4.

5.

6.

7.

PARAGRAPH

NAME _____ SCORE _____

DIRECTIONS   Using *classification* as the method of development, write a paragraph
on one of the following subjects. First, plan the paragraph; then compose the sentences for the paragraph. You may use facts found in the exercises of this book or
facts from your own knowledge.

SUBJECTS

1. categories or types of American housewives (or husbands)
2. categories or types of love
3. categories or types of modern marriages

CENTRAL IDEA

SUPPORTING POINTS

1.

2.

3.

4.

5.

6.

7.

PARAGRAPH

Paragraph practice

NAME _____ SCORE _____

DIRECTIONS   Using *comparison and/or contrast* as the method of development, write a paragraph on one of the following subjects. First, plan the paragraph; then compose the sentences for the paragraph. You may use facts found in the exercises of this book or facts from your own knowledge.

SUBJECTS

1. male and female behavior in infancy
2. marriage today and a generation ago
3. the woman who is committed to "the feminine mystique" and the woman who is "liberated"

CENTRAL IDEA

SUPPORTING POINTS

1.

2.

3.

4.

5.

6.

7.

PARAGRAPH

NAME _____ SCORE _____

DIRECTIONS   Using *cause and/or effect* as the method of development, write a paragraph on one of the following subjects. First, plan the paragraph; then compose the sentences for the paragraph. You may use facts found in the exercises of this book or facts from your own knowledge.

SUBJECTS

1. the causes (or the effects) of the high divorce rate
2. the causes (or the effects) of stereotyping male and female roles
3. the causes (or the effects) of the changed appearance of the modern male (or female)

CENTRAL IDEA

SUPPORTING POINTS

1.

2.

3.

4.

5.

6.

7.

PARAGRAPH

NAME _____ SCORE _____

DIRECTIONS   Write a paragraph on one of the following subjects. First, plan the paragraph; then compose the sentences for the paragraph. When you have finished writing the paragraph, list in the margin the type or types of development you have used.

SUBJECTS

1. a prediction about the future of marriage as an institution
2. new trends in masculine (feminine) appearance
3. how children contribute to (detract from) a marriage

CENTRAL IDEA

SUPPORTING POINTS

1.

2.

3.

4.

5.

6.

7.

PARAGRAPH

Individual Spelling List

Write in this list every word that you misspell—in spelling tests (see pages 95–102), in themes, or in any other written work. Add pages as needed.

NO.	WORD (CORRECTLY SPELLED)	WORD (SPELLED BY SYLLABLES) WITH TROUBLE SPOT CIRCLED	REASON FOR ERROR [1]
	considerable	con·sid'·er·a·ble	*a*
1			
2			
3			
4			
5			
6			
7			
8			
9			
10			
11			
12			
13			
14			
15			
16			
17			
18			
19			

[1] See pages 93–94 for a discussion of the chief reasons for misspelling. Indicate the reason for your misspelling by writing *a, b, c, d, e, f,* or *g* in this column.

a = Mispronunciation
b = Confusion of words similar in sound
c = Error in adding prefixes or suffixes
d = Confusion of *ei* and *ie*
e = Error in forming the plural
f = Error in using hyphens
g = Any other reason for misspelling

Individual Spelling List (cont.)

NO.	WORD (CORRECTLY SPELLED)	WORD (SPELLED BY SYLLABLES) WITH TROUBLE SPOT CIRCLED	REASON FOR ERROR
20			
21			
22			
23			
24			
25			
26			
27			
28			
29			
30			
31			
32			
33			
34			
35			
36			
37			
38			
39			
40			
41			
42			
43			
44			
45			

A
B
C
D
E
F
G
H
I

\